W9-CEH-183

YOUR
SOUL'S
ASSIGNMENT

CHRIS MICHAELS

Awakening World Enterprises
Kansas City, Missouri

Awakening World Enterprises (A.W.E.)
1621 West 50th Street
Kansas City, Missouri 64112

©2003 Chris Michaels

Cover design: Bense Garza, www.garza-artdesign.com
Front cover photo © 2003 Bense Garza
Back Portrait: © David Larson
Text Design & Typography: Jody Drake

Library of Congress Number is: 2003111103

Michaels, Chris, 1957–
Your soul's assignment / Chris Michaels

ISBN 0-9742256-0-6

Third printing, June 2006

DEDICATION

This book is dedicated to those who are searching
for meaning in life—to the people trying to find
their way through the dark.
Keep searching.
The light you're looking for isn't up ahead—
it's INSIDE of you!

CONTENTS

v

FOREWORD

The truth about life and death and God and reality is all over the place: in the scriptures of the world, the machinations of nature, and those "ah-ha!" moments and flashes of insight insinuating that the truth is in us, too. What's confounding about it is that truth speaks a language of spirit, a language few of us are educated to appreciate. Even those dedicated to making sense of it all are subject to the voices of media, culture, tradition, and practicality—noisier voices than those messengers of spirit. That's why we need interpreters, men and women blessed with the ability to package cosmic concepts in wrappings as clear and down-to-earth as a sheet of plastic wrap or a freshly cleaned window. Reverend Chris Michaels is such an interpreter.

I first heard Chris—we got past the Reverend stuff pretty fast—at his church in Kansas City, Missouri, in the mid-1990s. A friend said it would change my life. I was expecting a mere change of scene for a Sunday morning. When Chris ascended the stage— there was no pulpit; he's not a pulpit pastor—I sized him up as someone fully at home on earth: healthy and handsome, impeccably groomed and well turned out. "Okay," my cynical side silently challenged him, "You've got the image down. I dare you to come up with the substance." He did.

As a regular church-goer for most of my life, I have heard over 2000 Sunday sermons. I could tell you the gist of maybe half a dozen of them, and that first presentation by Chris Michaels I'll never forget. He was talking about our God-given right to be all that we can be. "You've got to get out and show the world what you can do," he implored us with a kind of intensity that let me know he wasn't just reciting a talk he'd written the previous Thursday; he was beseeching those present to reach inside themselves and draw out the wonder that could change the world. "Show it your talents," he continued. "And if you don't think you have any talents, stand next to somebody who has talent. If you don't believe that can work, I have two words for you:"—and then came a pause a good eight months pregnant—"Sonny Bono."

This was, of course, before Mr. Bono's untimely death, so the congregation exploded into laughter and spontaneous applause. My response was quieter: I changed on the inside. I knew at that moment that I had to get out and show the world my talents. I had to get my light out from beneath the proverbial bushel. Chris Michaels helped me do it—that day and in the years that followed. A great deal of the life I'm living today—a life that has brought to fruition a sizable stack of my dreams, and has me to the very brink of fulfilling the rest of them—I owe to the interpretive genius of Chris Michaels. In this book, you have that at your disposal, too. As the ancient yogis said, "When the student is ready, the teacher appears."

You may be an inveterate student of religion, philosophy, and metaphysics. Or perhaps this is your initial foray into the curious teaching that implies that God lives in you, as you, and, no matter who you are or what you have done, wants only the best for you. Whether you consider yourself a novice here or an old hand, I suggest that you read this book with an open mind and a willing spirit. If you find yourself arguing: "Not my life. I could never have it this good," keep reading. Chris Michaels is very convincing. And when the changes show up for you as improved health, financial stability, well-functioning relationships, and a peace that really does pass understanding, your own life will be more convincing still.

Victoria Moran,
Author of *Creating a Charmed Life:*
Sensible, Spiritual Secrets Every Busy
Woman Should Know

INTRODUCTION

This is NOT a self-help book! I don't believe in self-help books. They assume there's something *wrong* with you that urgently needs to be corrected, and then they profess to have all of the tools you need to create a perfect life. I guess if I were going to write a self-help book, it would be titled, *"I'm not okay, you're not okay—and that's OKAY!"*

In the Sixties when my mother would get overwhelmed, with her demanding career, raising three children and her unhappy marriage, she would turn off all of the lights in the living room and sit in the dark with her Whiskey Sour listening to Peggy Lee sing, *"Is that all there is? Is that all there is? If that's all there is my friend, than let's keep dancing. Let's break out the booze and have a ball...if that's all there is."*

Nobody has a perfect life! We all have challenges. We all have to make our own choices, and then reap the benefits, or suffer the consequences of those choices. So, this book isn't about *fixing* what's wrong with you. It's about trusting the wisdom that's already in you, enough to let it guide you.

Like my mother, sometimes we have to withdraw from the

daily activities of everyday life to find its real meaning and purpose. What are we here for? Are we here only to raise children and pay bills, or is there some greater purpose to our lives?

We live in a world full of confused people who do not understand the meaning or purpose of life. They are among the thousands of "walking wounded" that we share our world with every day. You see them driving to work angrily. They're the ones cutting you off in traffic, gossiping about you at work, and trying to compete with you for attention. They don't know that we are ONE people, on ONE planet, living in a universe created by ONE Life! They don't remember who they are, or where they come from. They have lost touch with their spiritual Source.

We each have an internal guidance system that can be trusted to the very end. That internal system is quite literally the presence of Spirit inside your soul. It has designed you specifically with a purpose and an intention. In other words, you are supposed to be doing something with your life; something significant and important!

I wrote this book to remind you of who you are (a spiritual being created for love). If it has come into your hands, you have already had some kind of *spiritual awakening*—and are looking for ways to fulfill your Divine potential. This book will help you with that. Follow its wisdom and you will live a simpler, freer life.

As you follow through the wisdom presented in the following pages—remember to give yourself time to assimilate new ideas and develop a new self-image. Be patient and kind to yourself as you are guided into a healthier, more successful life. And if this book helps to heal *your* life, then pass it on to someone else. The quality of life in the whole world improves every time one person awakens to their inherent power and potential!

Life is Good,
Chris Michaels

CHAPTER ONE

To Hell and Back...

My self-destruct button had been pushed so many times; the lettering on it had worn off!

When I was in my early twenties I was in the final phase of a self-destructive binge that began when I was only thirteen years old.

In seventh grade I smoked marijuana every day before and after school. And by the time I made it to high school, my drug of choice was "speed." I would take those little white-cross pills before typing class so I could type faster, or I would swallow a few in the evening and stay up all night smoking Marlboro cigarettes. When I started college I was into quaaludes and cocaine, mixed with several vodka shots every Saturday night—followed by a late drive home from the bar around 4:00 a.m.

And of course, as a result of this behavior, I had no *real* friends—no real joy—and no real life! When anything good would come my way, I would instantly push it away! And if anyone tried to love me, I'd quickly dismiss them—because that's what self-destructive people do.

I felt as though my life had a dark cloud hovering over it. I felt trapped inside my own story and too afraid to get out. So, I ran! I ran to so many different cities, I can't even remember all the places I lived.

I lived in Miami for a while and then San Francisco and even Biloxi, Mississippi at one point. And, I remember thinking to myself, "When I get to this new town no one will know me there, and I'll have a chance to start over." But it wasn't long before my life looked just the way it did in the last city.

And that's because I didn't know then what I know now— that wherever you go, you take your belief system with you and that is what creates your experience. So I found myself at the end of the self-destructive road rather quickly.

At the tender age of twenty-two years old, I was in my apartment in San Francisco lying in bed, near death, weighing less than a hundred pounds, with literally one friend left to me in the whole world!

And he came to visit me one day and gave me the best gift any friend has ever given me. He gave me the *truth*! He dropped it in my lap, walked out the door, and I never saw him again!

But as he left, his words kept ringing in my ears: "Chris, you're one of the brightest, most talented people I know and it's a damn shame you can't see that. But you've become so bitter and negative, that in order to protect myself, I have to bail out of this friendship. I hope you can find it in your heart some day to forgive me."

I sat there furious, with his monologue playing over and over again in my mind. Someone said: "The truth will set you free, but first it will piss you off." And I was really pissed! But underneath the anger was the pain I'd been trying to avoid feeling for years; the pain I was anesthetizing with drugs, sex and whatever else I could find to abuse.

Finally, as the anger subsided I started to feel that pain for the first time in my life. And it hurt worse than anything I'd ever felt! It was the pain of rejection, the pain of not being loved; the pain of self-hatred—and the horrifying fear that I was going to feel that way forever! I was terribly afraid that I would never find the love that my heart ached for and that I would never be completely accepted!

Finally, I heard a voice that sounded like it came from *outside* of me. And it wasn't the pleasant, sweet, little voice that spiritual people tell you one day you'll hear. It was a WARNING! The voice said: "Leave here—or die here!" It scared me so much that I sold everything I owned and left San Francisco in one week.

I was scared! I was lonely! I had no money, no friends and no answers. I was in search of some kind of spiritual wisdom that could heal my pain without insulting my intelligence. Being raised in a traditional Christian church I just couldn't relate to a judgmental old man-in-the-sky God, so I found a place in Atlanta, Georgia, where they taught that God is a Power for good in the universe whose only desire for our lives is to express goodness. They told me that Love is the grandest healing power on earth—and that I was loved unconditionally. They said that I had the power to change my life.

So, I listened anxiously and hopefully. And I started using my inherent God-power. I had years of experience using it unconsciously to destroy my life—but this was the first time I'd ever "consciously" used it for something constructive! I began by constructing a new belief system. I worked very hard to rid my mind of all of the pre-programmed negativity and to fill it with thoughts of self-worth and value.

And to be perfectly honest with you—I felt pretty hopeless and powerless! I didn't start out believing I was any good. I started out *wanting* to believe! But my *desire* to believe in a greater good for my life eventually led me into believing, and then finally, into *knowing*.

From that point on, my life started to turn around. I reached that wonderful turning point in consciousness where you work so diligently on faith and trust—and then finally one day, like a teeter-totter-you find yourself up in the air!

My new self-value brought me more money. My income doubled that first year as I reclaimed my life and my right to live it well. The next year, it doubled again. I found true friendship with honest people who really cared about me. For the first time in my life, I felt good about myself and hopeful about my future. My whole life transformed before my very eyes. It was miraculous!

And the best part of it all is—I know how it happened. It wasn't luck. None of it happened by chance. *It happened because I deliberately took my power back—power that was mine to use all along.* And I started using it affirmatively instead of negatively.

And then I reached a point where I wanted to help others do that as well. It's not enough to transform your own life and forget about the rest of the world. We're all part of a larger transformation—a global awakening to our power and potential as spiritual beings. And that's why I wrote this book—because I believe YOU have the power to transform your life too!

As a minister and counselor for the last thirteen years I have seen hundreds of people in similar desperate situations as I found myself. And the interesting thing is: We all have the same story. We've just got different characters and some of us have more chapters than others. But the *theme* of the story is the same; it's about finding your true, authentic self. It's about overcoming fear and finding the courage to pursue your dreams. It's NOT about fixing or repairing what's *wrong* with you. It's about restoring the good that's always been inside of you, waiting for your attention.

Your life is a Love Story waiting to happen. It's a transformation wanting to be revealed. Like the cocoon that's waiting to set the butterfly free—YOU are on the verge of becoming something you've never been. There's a greater good inside of you desperately wanting to come forth.

That's what your dreams are all about. They're not just

things you *hope* will happen some day. They are the coming attractions of your life, passing through your mind as signals of what life has in store for you when you find the courage to pursue them.

Someone said, "If you're going to go through hell, then go *through* it. Don't stop to buy property!" It's never too late to get started. No matter what hell you've been through, now is the time to get out. And the way out is the way *in*. The way to overcome your challenges and discover the life you were designed to live is to go *within* and find out who you really are.

CHAPTER TWO

Your Spiritual Needs

Lots of people wander aimlessly through life wondering if it has any purpose at all. They search near and far for answers and at some point they just give up—thinking it's all too complex to figure out anyway. So, they go through life bouncing from one experience to another, trying to avoid as much pain as possible.

I call this the "pinball" approach. Like the old pinball machines; one bumper throws you over to another, which bounces you back to yet another—until finally everything goes down the chute. And after awhile you get so used to being bounced around that it all seems *normal*. So even though you have high hopes that it will all work out "some day," you learn to lower your expectations to avoid as much disappointment as possible.

Many people live their entire lives this way, never stopping to think much about it. And others go through the mundane activities of daily experience with a peculiar sense of emptiness. Yet, there's "something" in each of us that suspects we are here for a more noble purpose than bouncing from one bad experience to another. *That "something" is our soul's assignment!*

Your soul's assignment is to discover, and then *uncover* the love you hold inside! Your soul was created by God to express love. So the only valid agenda worth pursuing in life is the peeling away of the layers of unhealed wounds and resentments so you can set your soul free to love again.

This is a huge challenge in a world full of "walking wounded." Every day we bump into people who are ignorant of their soul's only assignment—to love fully. Every day we are faced with negative messages about our identity and value. The world is full of needy people desperately looking for something to make them feel whole. But in spite of the obstacles of the human drama, we are here to heal our wounds, forgive those who've hurt us, and get on with life.

You were designed as an inlet and outlet for love—and you are not fulfilling the Creator's intention until you break down all of the "man-made" barriers that block love from entering your life. You were created out of God's desire for Self-Expression—and God is LOVE! So, everything you do that *invites* love into your life brings the Presence of God into the world. And everything you do that *blocks* love from entering your life restricts the Presence of God in the world. The primary purpose of your life, or your soul's assignment, is to be an open channel for love—allowing in, and letting out, God's Presence.

THE POPEYE AWARENESS

When I was a little boy I used to love to watch Popeye cartoons on television. Later, as I grew into a man, I figured out *why* I loved Popeye so much. Every Popeye cartoon has the same story. They are metaphoric for the challenges that we face in our journey through the human experience.

In every cartoon, Popeye is just going along, living his life, unaware that something big is about to challenge him. He's the nice guy, just trying to live each day without being bothered. But then, out of the blue comes Brutus—the bigger, stronger, meaner guy who unjustly abuses him.

At first he tries to ignore Brutus—just like we do when we're suddenly faced with something challenging. He politely stands aside giving Brutus the room he needs to make his presence known. But then as times goes on, Brutus invades more and more of his space unjustly challenging him on every occasion.

Finally, after he's taken abuse from Brutus over and over again, he reaches a point where he can't stand it one more minute! He gets to that place where we all eventually arrive—the point of power in our lives—the place where Popeye says: "I've had all I can stands, and I can't stands no more!" And that's when you hear the trumpets blare, the can of spinach opens, and Popeye's arms grow to the size of barbells.

Suddenly all hell breaks lose. He faces Brutus head on and fights his battle. Finally after putting Brutus back in his place, he wins the girl (Olive Oyl) and emerges triumphantly!

The story in the cartoon is a metaphor for our lives. We get up each day and go through the motions of everyday-life, assuming things won't change much. But then suddenly we're faced with a big challenge (Brutus)—or we just have that nagging feeling that something's not right.

At first, like Popeye, we just try to ignore it. "Maybe the bully will go away," we say to ourselves. "Maybe I'll be happier tomorrow in my job. Maybe the relationship I'm in will improve on its own. If I just ignore it, maybe it will all go away."

But the next day, Brutus is there again—that same annoying feeling of dissatisfaction is back again for a return engagement. Surprisingly, nothing changed overnight as we slept. So, we realize that inevitably we're going to have to DO something about it.

The first step is to face Brutus—the big, scary bully that's been haunting you. Stop trying to avoid him because each time you neglect him, he grows angrier and more annoying. Like Popeye, one day you'll get to the place where "you've had all you can stands and you can't stands no more." You may be at that place now. If so, good for you—that place is where your power begins!

The second step is to know what your Spirit needs in order to fulfill your soul's assignment. Just as Popeye needed the spinach to be strong, we need specific things to fulfill our assignment here on earth.

❧ YOUR SPIRITUAL NEEDS

The greater part of you is your *Spirit* and since it will outlast the body, investing in its care seems like the wiser choice.

This is what your Spirit needs in order to feel a sense of meaning and purpose—to fulfill your soul's assignment:

1. An intimate CONNECTION to a Higher Power
2. Regular and constant doses of LOVE and JOY
3. WORK that fulfills your Spirit's desire to contribute something worthwhile to life
4. SPIRITUAL GROWTH

Each of these needs will be discussed in detail in the next four chapters, but here is a brief overview.

❧ An Intimate Connection to a Higher Power

I don't care what the atheists say, everyone believes in something. We are not random errors in a cosmos that "accidentally" formed. Some "one" or some "thing" initiated life. You can call it God, The Great Spirit, Buddha, Creative Mind or George. It doesn't really matter because the name is not important. What's important is that YOU begin a relationship with it. (You may have noticed I use the word "it" as a name for God. Unfortunately, in the English language there is no word to describe something that is neither male nor female. And since I believe that Spirit encompasses the quality of both genders, in many references in this book, I have referred to God as "it." This was done deliberately to be inclusive, and is not intended to offend.)

The first gift of love is freedom. So, we've been given an individual life and then left free to make our own choices. We've been created, and then left alone to discover our Creator. In time, we all find our way home because the Creator placed a "homing device" within each of us. Our intense desire for love is that homing device and it will always lead us directly back to the one and only Source of unconditional love.

This Infinite Intelligence and Unconditional Lover is not a person whom you'll meet when your Spirit separates from the body. It's a Presence that is alive and surrounds you. God isn't a person, but a Presence. Yet since we've been set free to discover it for ourselves, we are responsible for our relationship with it. In other words, you have to make the first move. God has left the ball in your court.

Some people pursue their relationship with God in a mosque, church or temple. Others feel the Presence of God in nature, while others running track. We all have a unique way to *connect* and one way isn't better than another. Whatever causes you to feel God's Presence—do it! Talk to God. Go fishing with God. Run with God. Drive in the car with God. And do it regularly! Because the time will come when you really need to feel connected to that Presence—when you're faced with some big, hairy monster (or a Brutus) in your life and you are scared to death. And if you've taken time to connect to your Higher Power, you'll easily find the strength to overcome your fear and meet that challenge.

The first basic spiritual need is to connect to our Source (God)—to feel and sense a bond with a life-purpose greater than our own. We need to feel the Presence of a life greater than our own egos.

Regular and Constant Doses of Love and Joy

Without love, life has no meaning. And without laughter, there's just no reason to be alive. Your Spirit needs love and joy as much as your body needs food and water. In order to fulfill our spiritual needs, we have to keep finding new people to love and more reasons to laugh than to cry. Life is a series of roller-coaster events that lift us up just to drop us back down. It's not the ride that's harmful. It's when we take it too seriously that it becomes dangerous.

The world has too many old and bitter people in it—and it doesn't have to be that way. Life doesn't just automatically leave you angry and tired. You become that way after existing for too long without regular doses of love and joy. Without someone to love and something to laugh about, life can be really dreadful.

But once again, YOU are responsible for the quality of your own life experience. You have to find reasons to laugh and people to love. They're all around you if you just take time to look. People are hysterical and adorable! They're God's funniest and greatest creation. Dive in and take a chance. Introduce yourself to someone new. Find fun things to do like tap dancing or making pottery. Enjoy the Spirit in you and let it come out and play often!

Emmett Fox, in *Power through Constructive Thinking*, advised us to stop looking at the problem and start looking at the solution. When we give all of our attention to the things in life that upset us, we become upset. When we think about all of the injustices in life, we become bitter. If we feel hate, we become hate-full. But, if instead, we choose to feel love—by thinking about all of the things in life that are wonderful, then we become love-filled. It really is a matter of where you're looking and what you're choosing to give your attention to.

Do things that make you happy. Spend time with people who are fun. Dedicate your life to all of the people you love, and your Spirit will dance with joy!

Work that Expresses Spirit

As a spiritual being, you came into life with a special gift. There's something you can do that no other person can. That gift lies dormant within you, waiting to come forth until you find an outlet for it. In other words, you're not here to make a withdrawal. You're here to make a deposit. You're not here to get something good from life; you're here to give something good to life.

As spiritual beings, we need to know that we're part of something larger than our own ego-agenda—and that life has some greater purpose than buying groceries and making mortgage payments. Because inherently we sense that life is an ongoing process of creativity, we want to be part of creating something worthwhile. For many people, their work is an opportunity to do that.

Quit looking for a job and start listening for your calling. If you don't know what your calling is, go within and ask: "God, what am I here to do? What do I have to give to the world? How am I to spend my life?" And then listen and watch. Listen for gentle urgings. Watch for signs along the way that lead to your answer. When you're on the right path, Spirit will wink at you!

Spiritual Growth

"You, like all others, are seeking the joy of living. You wish to be needed, to be loved, to be included in the great drama of life. This urge is in every individual. It is in everything."

—Dr. Ernest Holmes, *This Thing Called You*

I don't think most people die of disease. I think they die of boredom! They stay in dead-end jobs because they're too afraid to quit. Their marriages are dispassionate and lifeless. They're on a merry-go-round of going to work, coming home, watching T.V., going to bed, waking up, and starting the whole boring routine over again. And their lives become so unfulfilling that finally one day, some obscure disease comes along and they use it as an exit strategy.

Without growth there is no life! We simply have to grow in order to stay alive. We hold *inside* of us an infinite potentiality and unless we find some way to release that potential, our soul remains unexpressed and we become very unhappy. That's why it's so important to find new challenges, create new projects, pursue old dreams and explore new possibilities. Staying interested in life feeds your soul. It's an absolute prerequisite for creative living.

A wise colleague of mine, Dr. Kennedy Shultz wrote: "The law of life is not a law of acquisition. It is a law of growth." Surely the Creator of the universe made us for something more important than owning a bunch of stuff!

We're not here to *get* things; we're here to *be* something! We're here to let out what we already possess inside. And as we do that, life becomes simpler. We encounter less conflict. We become less impressed with negative people and circumstances. We find ourselves less fearful. We grow beyond our previous experiences and become more powerful.

The words to an old Negro spiritual say, "Lord, I ain't where I *want* to be—but thank you Lord I ain't where I *used* to be." Inherently we all know that we can be more than we have been. We've had a glimpse of our inherent possibility. We've seen it in our dreams. All we really need is the courage to pursue our dreams. We need to know that Spirit is the power that can make our dreams come true. And then we need to *trust* that power to make it so.

Get out of your comfort zone! Try new things. You don't have to be good at it. The world won't end if you don't do everything perfect the first time. Challenge yourself to learn a new language, cook an exotic meal, give a speech, or go mountain climbing. Whatever you fear the most is what you must do. That's how you grow. That's how your spirit feels its aliveness!

CHAPTER THREE

A Intimate Connection with Spirit

YOU ARE A SPIRIT, NOT A BODY

"Your soul belongs to the universe. Your mind is an outlet through which the Creative Intelligence of the universe seeks fulfillment."
—Dr. Ernest Holmes

Philosopher William Irwin Thompson suggests that we are suffering from some kind of collective hypnosis that prevents us from seeing who we really are. "We are like flies crawling across the ceiling of the Sistine Chapel. We cannot see what angels and gods lie underneath the threshold of our perceptions." We look too closely at our lives and judge too quickly. We are more than we appear to be and far more capable than we've yet shown.

It's as if we're all seated in a grand arena looking at God. But since we each have different seats, we all see something unique, or perhaps a *different* angle that no one else can see. That's the conflict in our religions. We're all looking at God, yet the Christians see one particular aspect and the Jews another. The Muslims have their angle and so do the Buddhists. And each thinks that what they see is *right*—because they're looking straight at it. But the "thing" we're looking at (God) is much larger than we originally thought. It encompasses the perspectives of all world religions. It is more than we could have ever imagined!

That same truth applies to *your* life. You can look at your past experiences and create a negative opinion of your value. You can look at your current condition and access your worth. You can judge the value of your life based on the shape of your body, or the number of pages on your resume. But there is more to your life than what meets the eye.

There is much more to you than what occurs between the date on your birth certificate and the date on your death certificate. Your body is NOT who you are, and the reflection in the mirror has nothing to do with your worth.

You are an individualized expression of a perfect Creator who designed you specifically to be who you are! Every quirk of your personality, every angle of your perspective, every idiosyncrasy that makes up your unique character was *intentionally* created and assembled to make YOU! You have a unique way of being that no other person has, or ever will!

Inside every individual lies a Divine seed of infinite potential. That seed lies dormant until we awaken to the power and potential it holds for our lives. Because we are in some kind of collective trance that prevents us from seeing our true nature, the spiritual journey must first begin with an *awakening*.

Either through desperation or inspiration, we awaken to the memory held within us that life contains more than our personal experience. We then begin to peel away layer after layer of inherent potential until the seed is fully exposed. As a result of this process, our lives grow fuller and richer.

You are a spiritual being, not a human body! The true value

of your life has nothing to do with your body, how old it is, or what kind of shape it is in. The Spirit that created you is the Life Force within you. It animates your body and has given it to you as a vehicle for your soul's expression, for as long as you need it. When the time comes that your body no longer serves your soul, you will lay it down and move on with your life. You will leave your body behind with no more concern than you had for the old car you used to own.

Your life is NOT a mistake. God doesn't make mistakes. You were created for a reason and with an intention. There's something you're supposed to be doing with your life that will make a difference to others. Your Creator has placed you here at this time in history because you have something the world needs right now. It's time to wake up and realize the unique gift that only YOU possess.

You Are NOT...
Your body
Your income bracket
Your job, career, or position
Any role you play (father, mother, mentor, etc.)
Your address
Your education

We get thousands of messages each day from the people around us that the value of our lives comes from things *exterior* to our being. Turn on the television set and in a matter of minutes, our self-obsessed culture will tell you that your value comes from youth and beauty. Contrary to the thousands of messages we receive each day from our consumer-addicted culture, life is not about "stuff and things." Will Rogers said: "People spend money they haven't earned yet, to buy things they don't want, to impress people they don't like." Many people live their entire lives just trying to keep up with the Jones's next door. They risk their financial future for today's trinkets. They work too hard to buy things they don't really want or need. They're running as fast as they can to win the rat race. But as Lily Tomlin said, "The problem with the rat race is, even if you win, you're still a rat!"

Our value doesn't increase by owning the latest model car, or having the largest house. Neither does a resume show the true value of a human being. It's merely a list of companies and dates of employment. From a cosmic perspective, it doesn't matter whether you're a doctor or a dishwasher. Spirit isn't impressed with material assets, titles or degrees. It is only interested in creating new outlets for expression—and then expressing *through* them.

Yet, the world doesn't recognize you as a spiritual being. That's why it's so important to take time each day to remember that the value of your life doesn't come from anything *outside* of you. It doesn't come from the size or shape of your body. It doesn't come from how much money you have in the bank or what position you hold at your place of employment.

You are not your house, your degree, or social status. You are a spiritual being created by God, living in a spiritual universe governed by spiritual Law. You are a unique creation of a Perfect Intelligence, and your life is a once-in-a-lifetime opportunity to express who you are!

You ARE...
A spiritual being
A unique creation of God
Spirit individualized
A once-in-a-lifetime event
A powerful being
A co-creator
The one who makes a difference

THE KINGDOM OF HEAVEN IS WITHIN

"When Jesus said, 'The kingdom of heaven is within you,' he was saying that everything that you might need in life exists as a potentiality within you now."

—Eric Butterworth, *The Universe is Calling*

Many people believe that heaven is a geographic location with golden streets that you arrive at upon death—*if* you've been good in this life. But if we are to take Jesus' words as truth, then we know that no such "physical" location could exist.

The kingdom of heaven is a state of consciousness of self-awareness. It is a place we arrive at in consciousness when we are aware of our oneness with Life (Spirit).

When we choose to be a willing channel for Divine action, we do NOT *lose* our individuality in this oneness. In fact, just the opposite is true, we *fulfill* our individuality. We become our true selves!

By the choices we make everyday, we are creating our own world of experience. It can either be a "hell-on-earth" or a "heaven-on-earth" depending on what choices we make. When we choose to tap into our inherent potential and claim our good, we are entering a consciousness of heaven. When we live in fear and doubt, holding back what we have inside, we enter a consciousness of hell.

Every individual is left free to choose for themselves. The Bible says, "Choose today whom you will serve."

KNOW WHERE YOUR POWER COMES FROM

You are a powerful being living in a universe that is receptive to your individuality. What you think matters. Your ideas are important. Your perspective is invaluable. Your thought is creative.

The words you choose to speak either lift you up or put you down—but always the choice is yours! Life is, quite literally, what you make of it.

Your power is *internal.* It comes from the life of God *within* you, seeking expression *as* you. There is no external power source in your life, except what you have chosen to give your power to. No one has power over you! You have complete power over the quality of your life experience because you are the only person choosing how to act and react to any given circumstance. Your power lies in that choice. Between what happens to you (stimulus) and what you decide to do about it (response) is where your power lies.

Stimulus + Response = Your Personal Experience

CONDITIONED RESPONSES VS. CHOSEN RESPONSES

As a child, your parents, teachers and other authority figures taught you how to respond to many situations. You learned to respond to life much the way they did. Whether their responses were empowering or defeating was not something you had the wisdom to figure out at the time. However, as you mature, you must take time to reevaluate how you are currently responding to life. Are the choices you make truly *yours?* Or, are they just *programmed* responses that you learned years earlier?

Unfortunately, a very small number of people stop to ask these questions. Most people respond to life unconsciously with choices that were made for them a long time ago.

Here are some *conditioned* responses to every day occurrences:

Stimulus	Conditioned Response
Job loss	Anger, frustration. Go out and get drunk.

Divorce	Sense of failure and loss. Make the "other" person bad and wrong.
Someone is critical of you.	Loss of self-esteem.
Someone treats you poorly.	You treat them poorly.
Someone you love dies.	Depression, despair. A deep sense of hopelessness and helplessness.

Here are a few chosen responses to the same circumstances:

Stimulus	**Chosen Response**
Job loss	Use it as a signal from life that it is time to move on. Remember that every door closing, is another door opening. Start building a new dream.
Divorce	Know that the person you are leaving behind was just *one* opportunity for love in a universe filled with love. Forgive yourself and move on.
Someone is critical of you.	Know that other people's opinions are only as valid as *you* make them.
Someone treats you poorly.	You respond by setting loving boundaries that respect each of you as spiritual beings.
Someone you love dies.	Feel the loss, but do NOT desecrate their life by going into deep despair. Trust their choice, and know that their care is in God's "hands."

How you choose to respond to any circumstance creates your personal experience. You can have "knee-jerk" responses or self-chosen ones. Your power lies in what choice you make!

NOTHING WORKS LIKE AUTHENTICITY

Years ago I worked with a woman who started spreading rumors around the office about me. She was the kind of person who would be as sweet as candy to your face, but then as soon as you turned your back, out came the knife!

At first, I ignored it. But then, the rumors became more and more vicious. And it was very uncomfortable pretending to be nice to her, knowing what she was saying behind my back.

So one day I called her into my office and gave her the following monologue. I said, "I called you in here today to tell you that I don't like you! I want you to know that up front. I know we have to work together, and I can do that. I don't have to like you to work well with you. So, let's just be honest and stop pretending to like each other from now on!"

Needless to say, she was flabbergasted, but the rumors stopped that day! And to my surprise, before I left the company three years later, that woman had become one of my best friends!

Anne Morrow Lindbergh said, "The most exhausting thing in my life is being insincere." If every day you do the opposite of what you really want to do, and say the opposite of what you really think, you're bound to sacrifice both your sanity and your happiness.

Nothing works better than authenticity. It's the one thing we all want each other to be—*real!* So if you're truly a nice person, then be nice. But if you're not, at least be honest and upfront about your feelings. In the end, it will save us all a lot of grief.

TAKE OFF THE MASK

A lot of people pretend to be something they're not—because they're afraid that what they *are,* isn't good enough. So they pretend to have more money or talent than they actually possess. They imitate others who appear to have more than they do.

And their lives end up being a charade because "something in them" always knows the truth. That "something" is Spirit and it will continue to haunt them with feelings of inadequacy until they find their true, authentic selves. In the end, we must be ourselves!

Don't waste your life pretending to be something you're not. Take off the mask and let the world see the real you! Some will like what they see, and others won't. But your value doesn't come from other people's opinions of you. It comes directly from your connection to Spirit (God-within-you).

There is nothing sadder than a life half-lived—someone who has lived their entire life too afraid to speak their mind and express who they are. Don't be one of them. Take off the mask and trust that what Spirit created you to be is worth being!

You are ONE with All Life

"...within man is the soul of the whole; the wise silence; the universal beauty, to which every part and particle is equally related; the eternal one. And this deep power in which we exist and whose beatitude is all accessible to us, is not only self-sufficing and perfect in every hour, but the act of seeing and the thing seen, the seer and the spectacle, the subject and the object, are one."

—Ralph Waldo Emerson

In this essay, Emerson is trying to convey the ONENESS of our nature. We are not a *part* of God. God's Spirit has not been *divided* among us. ALL of it is equally present in each of us. Much like a holographic picture, where every part contains the entire picture, each of us is a center of God's power and potential.

We realize our oneness through our connection to each other. That is why our personal relationships are such a wonderful opportunity to experience this connectedness through shared experiences of love and joy. So it's not enough to know the value of who *you* are. It's equally important to know the value of *every* person you meet. Whether you are able to see it or not, every person has as much value to God as you do.

When you do your spiritual work, remember to include *every* person in your prayers. No one has to be sick in order for you to be well. No one has to lose in order for you to win. No one has to be poor for you to be wealthy. There is enough good to go around. God has an infinite supply of good for all of us.

THE GIFT OF LIFE IS NOT COMPLETE UNTIL YOU ACCEPT IT!

The "Giant" has awakened in YOU! The "Giant" is the Life of Spirit—and it is rising up within you so that you may know your true purpose and mission in life. You have come into this life to provide God an outlet for individual expression. You were created as an *instrument* of the Divine. You are here to receive the good that God has to give. And the only way you can do that is to have a consciousness (an awareness of your value) that allows you to accept it.

Spirit has given you everything you need to live a happy, ful-filled life. You have a mind that is tuned into an Infinite Mind which provides you millions of ideas and choices. You have the free will and determination of your individuality. You have a heart that will guide you to what is right and truthful. You are immersed in the presence of Spirit.

You have been set free on the sea of life with your own vessel. You are the captain of your own soul. You determine your worth. You define what has value. You decide what to create. This is the greatest gift that God gave you—the gift of self-determination.

Life will be to you whatever you are to it. If you give love, you will be surrounded by love. If you are generous with others, you will prosper beyond measure. If you honor yourself and respect others, you will attract wonderful people into your world. You will receive exactly what you put in to life. Each contributes his/her own consciousness—and each receives his/her own experience.

Live each day faithfully knowing this truth. Honor yourself—and everyone you meet as God incarnate—and your life will be truly blessed! Accept the good you've earned today, knowing you are worth it. And work to include a greater good for tomorrow. Open your heart to accept and give the love inside of you!

CHAPTER FOUR

Unchain Your Heart:
Regular Doses of Love and Joy

✳ Keep Your Eye on the Doughnut

When I was a kid my stepfather had an unusual saying that was supposed to remind us of a great truth. It went like this:

As you wander through life brother,
Whatever be your goal,
Keep your eye on the doughnut—
And not on the hole.

It's an annoying little saying and I'm not sure why I remember it, but I do. It wasn't until much later, in adulthood, that I was able to decipher the meaning of his little saying. It means that we should always keep our attention focused on the things that are the most important in life and forget about the rest.

If loving is our soul's main purpose and assignment in life, then we have to be sure we're making time and space for our most important priority. Clearing away our reasons and excuses as to why we're not worthy of love has to become our top priority. And then LETTING OUT the love we hold inside has to follow as a close second.

Be certain that you are living consciously and making choices that honor your soul's assignment to love. Make sure you're not wasting time on trivial pursuits. If your life is chaotic and filled with unsatisfying activities, start clearing out the things that no longer bring you love and joy.

Make love and joy your compass in life! Find people, work and activities that satisfy your heart's desire for love and joy. Love (and its by-product, joy) is the only thing that's really important. Everything else in your life should be rearranged to accommodate it!

When you come to the end of your life, the only thing you'll wish you'd done more of is to love. You're not going to wish you'd invested in stocks or climbed Mount Everest. You're going to regret not having loved enough.

I've seen many people at the end of their lives and the only thing that's important to them is to say, "I love you" to all of the people who've touched their lives. When all of our titles and dignities are stripped away, we are left with the only thing of true value in the whole universe—Love!

I've also known people who've gone through near-death experiences and they tell me when they arrived on the other side of the veil of human life, they were greeted by a loving Presence. And in a completely non-judgmental way, they were asked two questions: *"What did you learn?"* And, *"How much did you love?"*

If this is what really happens, we need to be sure we're living in a way that will allow us to answer those questions proudly. I don't know about you, but if I'm ever asked by my Creator, *"How much did you love?"* I want to answer: *"A whole lot!"*

Don't waste your life on trivial pursuits. Stop running through life dazed and confused. It's not about "stuff and things."

It's about love! It's always been about love! All of the lasting joy we receive in life comes from our loving relationships. Love is the first thing we want to *feel* when we enter this world, and the last thing we want to communicate as we make our exit.

I'M FROM EARTH, BUT MY FATHER'S FROM PLUTO

My mother tells me that when I was about five years old I looked my father straight in the eyes one day and said: *"Whatever I do in this life and whatever I become, I don't want to be like you!"* So that kind of tells you about my relationship with my father.

Try as we might, we just couldn't understand each other! And it seems like it started the day I was born. We had absolutely nothing in common, except a shared biology. And the older I got, the more resentful I became that he wasn't the father I thought he should be.

He was a simple, country boy—not the urban intellectual I aspired to be. He was a fearful man. I never once heard him talk about a dream, much less finding the courage to pursue it. And like many men of his generation he was emotionally absent— unable to express his feelings because of decades of social programming that told him that it's not what men do!

I, on the other hand, was passionate and expressive, courageous and adventurous! We were millions of miles apart on everything politically, socially—and certainly when it came to religion.

He and his wife are members of a very rigid, Christian denomination. And to this day neither of them has ever attended a single lecture, or read one word of anything I've written— and never expressed any desire to do so.

We never understood each other, ever! And for years I thought that meant we couldn't *love* each other either.

Like a lot of people, I thought *understanding* was a prerequisite to love. I thought you had to get inside someone's head and figure out *why* they do the things they do before you could love them. And God knows I tried with my father! We talked. We argued. We tried to reach some kind of consensus or agreement. But we could never find any common ground. So, the final strategy was to spend many years just trying to ignore each other.

And then one day, after many unsuccessful attempts at finding love in my own life, I attended a workshop. The facilitator, Dr. Kennedy Shultz, said two things that have stuck with me to this day. The first thing he said was: *"Until you heal the relationship you have with your parents, you're not really a candidate for loving anyone else."* And I thought to myself: "Oh great, now I'm really screwed! So that's why I haven't been able to attract anyone decent in my life!"

But then I was relieved to hear him say the second thing. He said: *"Understanding has never been a prerequisite for loving. You don't have to understand someone before you love them!"*

So I was making the same mistake everyone else makes with love—they try to put understanding *first*. But actually it works the other way around. If you love them first, you'll grow to understand them later. Love opens the way to understanding!

Ironically, the one thing I spent years, maybe even decades, trying to get from my father was his love and acceptance. I wanted him to accept me just as I am! And yet that's the one thing I wouldn't give him. I couldn't accept his politics or religion, or his emotional inabilities. I rejected everything he believed in because I just couldn't *understand* how he could be the way he was! The one thing I was trying to get from him—unconditional love and acceptance—was the very thing I was denying him—love without understanding.

And when I realized that, I stopped trying to understand him and just started *loving* him!

And today we have a well-healed relationship. Mind you, we still don't understand each other. And there are subjects we just don't go near! But there's a healthy respect for our differences and a genuine feeling of love in our hearts.

I share this success story with you because I think that all of the stories of our lives are really about finding our way to love. If God is Love—and we are created in Gods image and likeness—then all of our attempts to know ourselves and understand God, are really about learning how to love! Love is the soul's only assignment! Everything else is secondary and mostly irrelevant.

From God's perspective it doesn't really matter what kind of car you drive, or how big a house you live in. All of the things we think are important really aren't. They're just trivialities that are supposed to keep us amused while we learn to love. All of the pretty, shiny objects, the new cars and new clothes—and all the things we see in store windows and think we've just got to have, aren't the real priorities in life. Love is! In the end, the only thing that matters is: How much did you love? Did you grow in love? Did you learn something about love?

☘ OPEN HEARTS

"It is one of the ironies of relationship that no one else can open our hearts. We may have closed our hearts down to protect ourselves from others, but the truth is that we are the ones locked into our closed hearts. We are the ones who suffer from lack of trust and lack of freedom."

—Paul Ferrini, *Living in the Heart*

The world is full of people longing for love who have no real opening for it in their lives. They carry the heavy burden of past hurts, resentments and hidden agendas into every new relationship, making them poor candidates for love. They're suspicious of any kind or loving act someone shows them, and yet, at the same time are quite anxious to complain about how loveless their lives are. It's a sad contradiction for people to sit and wonder why they feel so lonely, yet watch them guard their resentments like precious metals.

We've all encountered people who simply cannot say, "I'm sorry. I was wrong." Their egos won't allow it! So they stand their ground and rationalize their position. Even if it means losing a friend or never speaking to a relative again, they maintain their rigidity with towering self-righteousness. Completely unaware of what they've really lost, they wake up one day and wonder why they're all alone.

For whatever reasons, some people would rather be *right* than be happy! People, who have been diminished or devalued excessively in life, perhaps through constant criticism from an authority figure in childhood, have a strong *need* to be right. They've been condemned so much that they just can't stand it one more time! They can't stand to make an error or be made to feel wrong again. So they absolutely insist on being right!

Our culture tends to glorify this neurosis and excuse it away as "perfectionism." Though people around them may say, "Oh, they just have high standards," the truth is: They're tormented souls who can't bear the slightest imperfection. They see each admitted mistake as a personal attack on their own integrity. And if this condition is left unhealed, the victims will create a life that spins in a vicious cycle of trying to be perfect and never feeling like they've done anything good enough. It is a life of self-torment and internalized hatred.

CHOOSE HAPPINESS OVER RIGHTEOUSNESS

Rabbi Harold Kushner tells the following story: A woman sees two children in a playground get into a fight. One of them says, *"I hate you! I never want to play with you again!"* For two or three minutes they play separately, and then they come back and start playing with each other again. The observer says to a woman sitting next to her, *"How do children do that?"* And the neighbor says, *"Oh, it's easy. They choose happiness over righteousness."*

Perhaps there's a valuable lesson to be learned in this story. Choose happiness over righteousness! Even if you're *right*, it's okay to let it go. In the end you won't remember what was so important that made you choose sides in the first place. All you will remember are the times you loved. And the only thing you'll regret are the times you didn't.

The only pain that tends to haunt us throughout our lives is the pain we feel for not loving. Every time we miss an opportunity to love, something in our heart feels a *permanent* loss. And since our soul's only assignment on earth is to love and be loved, each time that happens, something inside us cries out, "You have forsaken me again!" Something in us knows we've failed to fulfill our Divine purpose.

Get off your high horse and come down to the level we're all on. Everybody makes mistakes. Everybody gets hurt. It's okay to say, "I'm sorry." Commit your life to being *happy* and forget about being right! Reset your soul's agenda to love again, in spite of all of the reasons not to.

I WILL LOVE AND ACCEPT YOU WHEN...

Self-love and self-forgiveness are the first two steps in any healing process. Ironically, in order to get better, we have to accept ourselves exactly as we are right now—warts and all.

So much of the love and acceptance we give ourselves is conditional. We will accept ourselves when we lose ten pounds, or get a raise, or achieve our goals. But in order to truly heal our lives, we have to accept ourselves IN ANY CONDITION! We have to come to a place where we are acceptable no matter what shape our finances, relationships, or bodies are in.

My dog Nicholas taught me about self-acceptance. One morning I awoke from a restless night's sleep, staggered to the mirror and said out loud, *"Oh my God, how can so much damage take place overnight? All I did was lie down for eight hours!"* I thought I looked old and tired. And then I noticed Nicholas, at my feet, looking up at me wagging his tail. He didn't care about my morning-breath. He didn't care how old I was. He didn't like me better when my hair was combed. HE LOVED AND ACCEPTED ME EXACTLY AS I WAS!

Isn't it interesting that dog spelled backwards is God? I think God loves and accepts us exactly as we are right now. God's love is unconditional! And if the power that created the universe has the good taste to love us unconditionally, then why shouldn't we?

Start today by affirming, *"It is okay for me to be in ANY shape. I love and accept myself exactly as I am right now!"*

Giving yourself love and acceptance today insures a future of greater joy and ease. It creates a consciousness that attracts others who will know how to love and accept you exactly as you are.

❉ OUR DESIRE FOR LOVE EXCEEDS OUR CAPACITY TO RECEIVE IT

A few years ago I counseled a man who came to me upset over a lost love. He was in a relationship with a woman whom he described as his "soul mate." They were together for about six months and things were going great. There was talk of marriage, children and buying a home together.

And then all of the sudden, she dumped him without any apparent reason. He was heart-broken and confused! Finally, after a couple of months he ran into a friend who also knew this woman and told him: "That's what she does to every guy she meets. She stays with them for awhile, gets really close to them— and then gets scared and runs away!"

I hear this same story from a lot of people. They meet someone and things are going great for awhile. And then all of sudden, without warning, they make a run for it, or do something ridiculous to sabotage the relationship. And when that happens, they always want to know *why*. Why did this happen to me? What went wrong?

Here's the reason why: People dart out of relationships fearfully because they don't have enough self-value to accept the love that's being offered. Perhaps they're able to effectively *give* love and get somewhat close to *receiving* it. But the closer they get, the more it challenges them to accept a love they just don't feel worthy of. That's because many people's *desire* for love exceeds their capacity to accept it!

To some degree that's true for all of us. Our *desire* for love goes way beyond what we're actually ready to receive. And it's always going to be that way because the amount of love that's available to us is eternal, everlasting and unconditional!

Your soul's assignment here on earth is to prepare the way for that love; to create a place in your heart to receive it. Your job is to let yourself be loved, in spite of all the things you've done that you think are so terrible! And the only way you're going to let that happen is to forgive yourself first.

To say: *"I did the very best I could with what I knew at the time—and now it's time to forget the past and stop using it as an excuse to limit my future."*

Forgiveness clears the way for love and opens your life to a greater good. It gets everything out of the way and lets the love in. When we forgive ourselves, we open our hearts to Spirit and our lives to a greater good. And when we forgive others, we're finally on the threshold of seeing life for what it truly is: One perfect Spirit expressing itself in an infinite variety of souls!

Self-forgiveness is the first step in creating a close relationship with God. We have to feel *worthy* of a Love that's unconditional and eternal or we'll never be able to accept it. And we'll never feel worthy until we first forgive ourselves.

Here's how you do that:

1) Start by trusting that what God made you to be is good enough! If the Infinite Mind that knows the mathematical equation necessary to initiate a universe went to all of the trouble to create you, why not trust that it knew what it was doing? Try to see yourself as God sees you—as another means of perfect expression, an inlet and outlet for Divine Love.

2) Then once you've got a good grip on that idea, and you stop beating yourself up and putting yourself down, start using your spiritual power constructively instead of abusing it. Treat yourself like somebody you love! Spend time thinking about the things you do well and the times you show love and compassion. Resist the temptation to abuse yourself over past errors. Show some self-kindness by giving yourself a break.

3) Then give the same gift to others that you just gave to yourself— Forgiveness!

And here's where it gets hard! It is one thing to think of yourself as a perfect expression of God and quite another to see your "ex-husband" or "ex-wife" as one. It is one thing to forgive yourself for the harm you've caused, but when you're on the *receiving* end of that harm, it's a little harder to let go of the pain!

And it's a giant leap from there to move beyond seeing your personal enemies entitled to God's love, to see everyone on earth entitled to love. What about the people who've hurt millions? Are they just as entitled to God's love? Was Hitler entitled to God's love? Is Osama bin Laden?

The answer to the question is yes. EVERYONE is included in God's love! Everyone is forgiven for everything! I know how difficult it is to conceive of a love that perfect, or unconditional, that it could forgive these men who've done such horrible things.

Can you imagine how God could forgive them? I would

have a hard time forgiving someone who hurt my dog, much less someone who killed other people. I have a hard time forgiving *myself* for the dumb things I do, much less for someone who took the lives of innocent people.

But no one is separate from God's love! No soul has been abandoned by love. That's why forgiveness is the most phenomenal gift of Spirit. It goes beyond human comprehension—that a love could exist that could forgive so much!

The only way I can understand it is to consider what you hear people say about love. They say: *"Love is blind!"* And I don't think that's true. I think just the *opposite* is true. Love grants us perfect vision. It's not that we don't see what's wrong with the people we love. We see "through" their faults and idiosyncrasies to the perfect Spirit within them. Love gives us insight into their Divine potential. It allows us to see through the veil of human error.

And if it does that for us—if it allows us to see ONLY that which is perfect and whole in each other, then maybe that is the way God sees each one of us. It sees beyond the hurt and pain of the human experience. It sees beyond our ignorance and shame, straight through to our heart and soul.

God sees us as we truly are: Its own special, unique creation, longing to be loved and accepted, wanting more than anything to be understood! And perhaps that's why God is able to forgive us: Because the only thing it really knows about us is the absolute truth of our being. God isn't impressed with our transgressions. It doesn't know about our sins!

God can easily dismiss our faults, just as we can for the people we love so dearly. To us, they're perfect. Even if they are kind of goofy to the rest of the world, we still love them. And to God, we're perfect—even though we may not be able to see it right now.

So start creating a self worth that can accept that Divine, perfect love by forgiving yourself today. And then, extend the gift of forgiveness to everyone around you.

❧ SELF FORGIVENESS

"The final mystery is oneself. When one has weighed the sun in the balance, and measured the steps of the moon, and mapped out the seven heavens star by star, there still remains oneself. Who can calculate the orbit of his own soul?"

—Oscar Wilde

Every judgment we have of someone else shows us some aspect of ourselves that we have not yet learned to accept and love. Inevitably, we come face to face with our own heart. We are the ones who must forgive ourselves.

No one is able to go through life without hurting someone. We make mistakes. We hurt others, sometimes intentionally and sometimes not. Since Spirit-IN-us knows that we're all ONE and that what we do to others, we also do to ourselves all forgiveness has to start with SELF-forgiveness.

When we were children, most of us had higher standards for our parents than they could meet. We expected perfection and were shocked to find that they were somewhat less. But as we grew and matured and made our own mistakes in life, we realized that no one is perfect. And our maturity allowed us to look back at our childhood and forgive our parents for not knowing everything, for being human and making human mistakes.

We have to take that same forgiving look at our own lives. We made the mistake of hurting others because at the time we didn't know any better. If we'd have *known* better, we would have *done* better. Everyone is doing the very best they can at any given moment in life. We're all operating at peak capacity with the current understanding we possess. That's why it's always appropriate to forgive yourself for what you didn't know.

You are paid in full for all that you've done in life, both the good and the bad. Nothing in the universe is holding a grudge against you or waiting to punish you at some later date. Reward and punishment are NOT God's game; unconditional love and acceptance *are.*

It's time to forgive yourself—to let go of the self-degradation and condemnation. And it's time to start loving again.

What Are You Waiting For?

I have a close friend who considers herself overweight because she doesn't look the same at fifty as she did at sixteen. And she has this boyfriend who loves her to death! It's so obvious when you see them together. He's kind and gentle to her. He opens the door for her. He actually listens when she talks, which few men do. But she refuses to have intimate relations with him because she says: *"I just don't feel right about my body. I'm too embarrassed to take my clothes off."*

She hasn't been intimate with anyone in at least a decade! So I said to her: *"What if it's going to be this way your whole life? What if you're just going to be this size? Are you going to live your entire life denying yourself love, just because you don't think you look good naked? Honey, nobody looks good naked! That's why God made Armani."*

Don't spend your whole life not letting yourself be loved over some stupid triviality like fat cells. Who cares? Take your clothes off and run through the house screaming: *"Baby, come and get me!"* Or else, you're going to get to the end of your life and have an awful lot of regrets!

One day you're going to have to face your Creator and when God asks: *"Why didn't you let yourself be loved?"* The only answer you'll have is— *"Because I was twenty pounds overweight!"* And how embarrassing will that be?

It's not important how you look, or how much you weigh. All that's really important is how much love and joy you let in to your life. So my advice is: Abandon yourself to love. Let go of your ego and your low self-estimation—and for once in your life, just trust that what God made is perfect!

❧ THE GIFT OF FORGIVENESS

You are a perfect expression of Spirit entitled to a life of love and joy!

If every person knew they were loved and accepted by God exactly as they are right now, the world could be instantly transformed! The power of that acceptance and the sense of safety it brings could change people's lives overnight.

The most powerful thing in the world is a person who knows they are loved—and the healthiest person in the world is the one who, in their own mind, knows they're okay no matter what anyone else thinks or says!

One of the great ills of our society and the cause of most of the violence and injustice in our world is that so many people feel unworthy of love! They don't think they deserve to be happy or live well because it's been pounded into their heads for so many years that they're not good enough, or that somehow, God is offended by the way they live or something they've done. And nothing could be further from the truth!

The truth is: You are a perfect expression of Spirit created out of God's love for itself with every right to express all that you are! And that's true for you and for every person who's ever lived. Close your eyes for a minute and say these words out loud and see if you can feel them and know that truth for yourself.

"I am a perfect expression of Spirit entitled to a life of love and joy."

So now the question is: Do you really believe it? Or do you hear the critic's voice inside your head saying: *"Yeah right! Sure you're perfect, all right! What about that last divorce? And what about the time you hurt your best friend?"*

Self-acceptance has to begin with *self-forgiveness* because we're all keenly aware of our own past mistakes. Accepting God's unconditional love begins first by forgiving yourself. That's why the Lord's Prayer says: *"Forgive us God, as we forgive those who've trespassed against us."* We are forgiven AS we forgive! In other words: God can't forgive us until we forgive ourselves!

The fact is: You have hurt other people. You've rejected their love. You've made fun of them. You've discounted their potential and ignored their gifts. You can't get through the human experience without making mistakes. You don't come into a world of six billion people who are all different from one another and not step on a few toes. And some of the harm you've done was completely unconscious. In fact, most of it was. But other times it was totally deliberate.

Nonetheless, ALL of it is forgivable! Everything you've ever done to harm yourself or hurt another person is forgivable. In fact, from God's perspective, it's already forgiven.

It has been written that "to err is human, to forgive, divine." That means that as long as we're in these human bodies, we're going to make mistakes. We can't avoid it. It's part of the human experience. But we are more than these mortal shells we carry around every day. We are *spiritual beings* with a Divine heritage! And that's our true self—the Higher self that allows us to forgive. That's the presence of God in us saying: *"None of it really matters! All there really is, is love—and the times when you didn't know that, aren't really important!"*

How Can I Forgive What Happened?

The first thing to know is that ANYTHING can be forgiven. Forgiveness is always the right choice, though it may be the greatest personal challenge. Forgiveness is an act of *self-love*. It is a statement to oneself that says: *"I want to move on with my life. I don't want to wake up hurting every day. I'm tired of being angry and resentful. I want to let it go!"*

We don't forgive because the person who hurt us *deserves* our forgiveness. We forgive because *we* deserve it. We deserve to live healthy, productive lives. We deserve to live free and happy. We deserve to NOT be one of the "walking wounded."

There are no "how-to steps" for forgiveness. And, there's no way to "work" on forgiveness either. The only way to forgive is to first be WILLING to forgive. Your willingness opens the way for the grace of God to enter your life and forgive.

Here's how it works: If you remain open and WILLING to forgive—you'll wake up one day and the forgiveness will have already taken place. Somehow, the grace of God "sneaks" into our lives and allows forgiveness to overtake our pain.

You'll know you've forgiven when you can recall the hurtful event—and have NO EMOTIONAL ATTACHMENT TO IT! When you talk about it, it will be as if you're giving an emotionally-detached report of events that once took place. That's how you'll know that you have truly forgiven.

All it takes is your *willingness* to begin. If you stay in a state of willingness—everything else will be taken care of for you. It's really just that simple!

Each time the hurtful event comes to mind; remain calm. Say to yourself: I am WILLING to forgive them. It's over, and I am ready to get on with my life!

❋ AN AMAZING STORY OF FORGIVENESS

Twelve years ago, in my very first year of ministry, a woman who had just been checked into a psychiatric hospital called my office requesting a visit. And from the moment I saw her face, I could tell she was in intense emotional pain.

As we sat and talked, she told me about her terrifying child-hood. Both of her parents were members of a satanic cult that sexually and emotionally abused their children as part of their sick ritual. The very people, who were supposed to be responsible for loving and protecting her, beat and raped her throughout most of her childhood.

And there she sat before me in tears, with so much pain in her heart that I began to feel it in my own. She looked me straight in the eye and asked: *"How I can forgive this? How am I ever going to move beyond it?"*

I didn't know what to say, so I sat there and cried with her. I couldn't heal her pain, but I could share the burden of it. I apologized for the way she was treated. I assured her that she deserved better. I promised her that it was possible to heal and move beyond her past, and the only way was through forgiveness!

So we sat and prayed together for forgiveness. I prayed to know that God's Love is so powerful that it can heal every hurt. I knew that God's presence inside her soul already knew how to forgive. I prayed for healing and forgiveness, and for her life to be restored to joy and ease. I never prayed so hard in my life as I did that day with her! And a miracle happened. God in me touched and saw God in her! The Divine in each of us acknowledged our presence and desire for its love. And by the time I left there, two hours later, I knew beyond a doubt that she would be completely healed!

About a year later, I received a card from her in the mail. She had fallen in love with a man and was married. She found the love and acceptance that she never got from her parents and healed her life through forgiveness. Her *willingness* to forgive and her sheer determination to live a decent life regardless of her past helped heal her emotional scars.

To this day, she is my hero and my example. Whenever I'm faced with something or someone I want to forgive, I think of her.

If after all that she went through, she can find *her* way to forgiveness; I guess I can too.

I don't know why things have to happen as they do. I don't know why people get abused and millions die in wars. Hell, I don't even know why bad things happen at all. But I do know there's a power for good in the universe seeing that everything comes out well in the end. And that power can, and will, forgive everything!

UNEXPRESSED LOVE

I have a friend whose father died five years ago leaving him absolutely grief stricken. He was the type of man who found it impossible to say, *"I love you."* So, he allowed his father to slip from this life without having said those three simple words. As the years passed, his grief turned to a depression that eventually led him to consider taking his own life.

Tormented by regret, he entered what some people call the "dark night of the soul." And it was during this period, with the guidance of a spiritual teacher that he learned the power of unexpressed love.

Love *expressed* brings joy and happiness! But love *unexpressed* brings pain and regret. It festers in our soul and begins to rot at the core of our being. It turns to neurosis and dis-ease and eventually infects every relationship we have. When we don't find functional ways to express the love we hold in our hearts, our lives become mundane and meaningless. Our soul knows the only thing worth living for are the times and the people we love. And without love, life isn't really worth a damn!

My friend eventually learned to express the love he felt for his father, even though he had already passed from this plane of existence. Love doesn't have any limits. It's not restricted by time and space so it's never too late to say, "I love you." By expressing the love he felt for his father, he was able to restore mental and spiritual health to himself and get his life back on track. And he said that his experience not only brought him closer to love, it also filled him with a new gratitude for his father. It seems there was one more lesson Dad had to teach his son—and that was the power of unexpressed love.

Unspoken Words and Uncried Tears

I was in a fancy restaurant the other evening having dinner. And I noticed a handsome family seated at the table next to me. The father and mother were impeccably dressed—and their young daughter had on a beautiful, crisp, new dress that looked like an entire can of spray starch had been spent on it. She looked as though she was about ten years old.

To amuse the little girl, the waiter provided crayons and a paper placemat for coloring. As she sat there coloring away, the waiter delivered a pink, fruity drink. A few minutes later my conversation was disrupted by a screaming, crying little girl. As I turned to look at the table next to me, I realized what happened.

The little girl's drink had been spilled all over her new art project and down into her lap on the crisp, new dress. And she was wailing and crying! Her emotional outburst was so dramatic, you'd of thought it was the end of the world! She just could NOT compose herself.

As I continued to watch, I noticed how uncomfortable the parents were becoming. They kept trying to hush the little girl. They whispered in her ear telling her, "This isn't the time and place for that kind of thing—so please be quiet." They did everything they could to stop the girl from crying, but nothing would console her. By God she was going to have her crying jag whether it was socially acceptable or not!

A few minutes later, after the mess was cleaned up and dinner was served, she was laughing and smiling again. Apparently a large dose of chicken fingers and fries was all that was needed to restore her joy and allow her to leave her disappointment behind.

Watching this scene made me wonder how much healthier all of us might be if we just let the tears flow, like the little girl did, when we are faced with life's disappointments. To hell with social correctness! What if we just bawl our heads off the next time we're sad?

I'm convinced that the leading cause of misery in the world is because thousands, perhaps even millions, of tears have *not* been cried! We hold on to too much pain. We have too many words left unsaid.

It's not what happens today that ruins our lives. It's what happened yesterday, last year, or when we were ten years old that we still have lodged in our heart. It's the pain of a disturbing childhood that we never got over, or some terrible loss that we never allowed ourselves to completely mourn.

One of the challenges of a spiritual being living a human experience is in going through the dramas of human life and finding some way to get through it all without suffering. We are not here to suffer. That was never God's plan for its beloved creation. We are here as spiritual pioneers who are set free on a cosmic adventure. We have been designed to go far and fast! And two of the things that slow us down and severely limit our growth are unspoken words and uncried tears.

When we don't communicate our true feelings to one another, a clog is created in consciousness that limits the soul's progress. And when we have unexpressed hurt or pain that we haven't taken time to process through our feelings, a deep sorrow begins to fester in our heart that limits whatever joy we can get from life.

To maintain health and wholeness, Nature demands movement. Everything in the universe is in motion. The water flows, the wind blows and the galaxy spins. Even your own blood has to circulate in order for your body to be healthy. This same truth applies to our emotional health. Emotions were created to allow us to process our feelings. They are to be EMOTED—or let out. When we're in pain, we're supposed to cry! We're supposed to feel our sadness and loss so we can move through it quickly and get on with life.

This wonderful Spirit that we each have inside of us DEMANDS expression! And our greater health and greater good in life comes from letting it out. Trying to put a stopper on it won't work. Pretending that you don't have time for the pain or finding some excuse to delay mourning a loss will only make matters worse.

Say what you need to say to whomever you need to say it. Cry your tears. Feel the loss. It won't kill you. In fact, just the opposite will happen. It will HEAL you!

What the World Needs Now Is Love Sweet Love

I've always found it rather peculiar that whenever something bad happens in the world how anxious everyone is to blame God. You hear people say, *"Why did God allow the holocaust? Where was God when those planes hit the World Trade Center? How can He just sit there doing nothing, in the midst of such tragedies? And what about the thousands of children dying of starvation in Africa each day—why does He let this go on?"*

And yet no one ever asks, *"Why does the earth spin in the precise orbit necessary to sustain life? Why do people fall in love? How do people heal? Where do we get the five billion new cells our bodies need each day just to stay alive? Why does each snowflake have a different design and every person a different gift? Who put the fragrance in a rose? What mind conceived of the millions of different species? Who created color and light? And where did we learn to laugh?"*

The answer to these questions can be found *within* you.

Because the Spirit that created you lives within you, and resides within all living things. God isn't an uncaring, distant deity waiting for judgment day to take action. God is a LIVING PRESENCE activated by your thoughts and feelings. God isn't a loving being. God is Love, itself—and every time you choose to love, you activate this Presence in the world.

We are responsible for the quality of our own lives! We are responsible for what happens on planet Earth. We have been given dominion and free will to make any choice. We are letting the children die in Africa. And we are causing the wars by having too many hearts filled with hatred instead of love.

I know how reluctant people are to assume responsibility for their own lives, much less for the conditions present in the entire world. It's much easier to look up in the sky and blame someone else. Sometimes, it really is more convenient to remain a *victim* of random forces that we pretend not to understand. After all, what can "little, ole me" do to change the world?

Here's what "little, ole you" can do: You can create a life worth living. You can set an example by the choices you make. You can choose to love instead of hate. You can try to understand others, instead of discounting or dismissing them. You can practice forgiveness. You can make love the main priority of your life. You can create a life that is so filled with love that everyone around you will be healed in your presence. That's how we change the world, one life at a time!

YOU are an important part of God's plan. YOU have something valuable to contribute to life. Spirit is calling YOU into action. So, stop being a victim and stop pretending the choices you make don't matter. Wake up and take your power back—and then learn to use it to heal YOUR life first, and then leave your healing imprint on the world.

CHAPTER FIVE

Spirit Is Calling:
Work that Expresses Spirit

CALLINGS

Like the pull of the sun on a flower, which causes the blossom to open and turn toward the light, Spirit is urging you to a greater life. It is an inner voice that says, *"This is not good enough. I made you for something greater. There is a better way for you to live."*

Too many people are pretending to be something they're not—because deep down inside they don't believe they're good enough as they are. Too many people are living in fear of their best ideas, instead of passionately and courageously pursuing them. Unfortunately most people aren't aware of their spiritual heritage or the extraordinary talent they possess. They're living lives that are half-expressed.

Spirit created you to be exactly who you are and for you to remain true to your self! It fashioned your unique personality and provided your special gift—and it lives as close to you as your next breath. Spirit needs you as much as you need it. You were created as an outlet for its never-ending supply of good. You were made to receive the gifts of life, love, and joy.

Spirit is calling you to live an *authentic life*—to be true to your talent, and to speak your mind. It is calling you to live honestly and act courageously, to be yourself, and to give your unique gift to life. Your *calling* is personalized and persistent. It may show up as a reoccurring dream, or a sudden urge to pursue a new career. It may be an inner knowing that a relationship has reached an ending and it's now time for change. However it shows up, it is trapped spiritual energy wanting to be released—calling on you to set your spirit free.

Gregg Levoy, author of *Callings*, says that, "calls are essentially questions. They aren't questions you necessarily need to answer outright; they are questions to which you need to respond, expose yourself, and kneel before." They may come in one or more of the following ways:

- A dream that keeps coming back, or what it is that pursues you in dreams;
- A symptom that recurs and is exquisitely metaphoric, such as a pain in the neck from shouldering too much responsibility;
- A conversation you overhear in a restaurant that seems as though it was spoken directly to you;
- Places in your life where there's friction. As in nature, friction occurs where changes are taking place or trying to;
- Song lyrics you can't get out of your head;
- Instructions that arise unbidden from the silence of meditation;
- What you would preach about if given an hour of "prime time;"

What if I Don't Know What to Do?

"It may be that when we no longer know what to do we have come to our real work, and when we no longer know which way to go, we have begun our real journey."

—Wendell Berry

Not knowing what to do is a call to find out what to do—not a message to STOP doing. We have within us an infinite well of wisdom and knowledge. We can tap into that wisdom by being open to receiving our call. When we stop saying, *"I don't know what to do,"* and start saying, *"Something in me knows exactly what to do,"* then we are opening ourselves up to that wisdom being revealed.

Stop running around asking everyone's opinion as to what to do. Go directly to the Source of all wisdom. Ask Spirit-within-you to reveal its intent and purpose for your life. And then go somewhere and be still—and allow its wisdom to rise to the surface of your conscious knowing.

When you're at a point of indecision in your life and you don't know what to do, take time for inner reflection and consultation with Spirit. It's not a time to make random choices. It's always better to wait and do nothing, rather than take action in fear and confusion. Wait until you have a clear understanding of your calling.

Also, know that: Only the *first* step will be revealed! Don't wait until you see the entire road before you act. When you know what the first step is: TAKE IT. As you do, the next step will be revealed. Spirit calls on us to trust as we're guided toward our fuller expression. We're not shown the whole road—only one step at a time! And that's a good thing. Because if you saw every step you are going to take, it would scare the hell out of you.

Five Questions to Help Expose Your Calling

1. What is the one thing you could stop doing, start doing, or do differently—NOW—that would most improve your life?
2. Who are your role models?
3. What is your heart's deepest desire?
4. What idea keeps coming to mind, year after year?
5. At the end of your life, how would you like to be remembered?

WHEN YOU'RE ON THE RIGHT PATH, SPIRIT WILL WINK AT YOU

"Too often we travel on cruise control, and the events of our lives flick by like white lines on the freeway, their lessons lost on us."

—Gregg Levoy, *Callings*

In *Hymns to an Unknown God*, San Keen instructs us to "enter each day with the expectation that the happenings of the day may contain a clandestine message addressed to you personally. Expect omens, epiphanies, casual blessings, and teachers who unknowingly speak to your condition."

When you're delayed in traffic or stuck in line at the grocery store, look around to see what messages might be there for you. Listen to conversations going on around you. Watch for signs. Spirit is communicating with you in a thousand different ways every day. We are surrounded by messages from the Divine!

So, pay attention! When you're on the right path, Spirit will "wink" at you to let you know.

ROSES NEED TIME TO OPEN

I have a friend who was throwing an elaborate party on Valentine's eve. The day of the party, she went to the florist and spent a fortune on flowers. At the entrance of her house was a grand foyer where she had strategically placed a beautiful, round antique table. On special occasions she would place a crystal vase filled with long-stemmed red roses perfectly centered in the middle of the table.

As she arranged the flowers an hour before the party she realized the roses hadn't opened, so she filled the vase with warm water to encourage them and then hurried upstairs to get dressed. When she came down, the rosebuds were still closed as tight as a fist. So, without thinking, she *forced* them open, pulling on each petal to make them bloom.

When guests arrived at the house that evening, they were greeted by a beautiful vase filled with a hundred dollars worth of limp, ugly roses!

The message of this unfortunate saga is that nature has its own time and place for our callings to emerge. They cannot be *forced* or scheduled for our own convenience. They have to come forward just as we are strong enough and courageous enough to pursue them.

Do you remember a time in your life when you tried to *force* something to happen that wasn't ready to happen? What were the results? How many times have you tried to *make* things happen that weren't ready to happen on their own? How did your experience leave you feeling?

Be gentle. Allow Spirit to express through you in its own way and time. Meditate daily on being receptive to what it wants to express in your life. Listen to special messages or urges that arise from within—and then trust your inner guidance. Be patient! Sometimes your callings will come in flashes of inspiration, through "dark nights of the soul," or through dissatisfaction.

☀ IT'S OKAY TO BE DISSATISFIED

Nothing is wrong with you because you're dissatisfied with your life. Dissatisfaction can be very beneficial to the creative process. It's usually the starting point for something new. Being dissatisfied with an area of your life doesn't necessarily mean you're an unhappy person. I am very happy with my life—but there are several areas with which I am dissatisfied.

Someone said the greatest temptation in life is to settle for less than what you really want. It's very tempting to accept less than what you really want and then find yourself dissatisfied later. I counseled a woman once who told me the moment she was walking down the aisle to get married, she knew she had settled for less than what she wanted in a mate. Predictably, her marriage didn't last long.

Whenever we accept less than what we really want, that nagging voice of truth never seems to shut up. Week after week, month after month, it gets louder and louder until finally it screams in your head: "GET OUT!"

Here are some questions to ask yourself:
- Where is your dissatisfaction?
- What area of your life have you accepted less than what you really want?
- What problem keeps repeating itself over and over again?
- What truth do you already know about your life, but keep trying to pretend isn't real?

Many people sit with their dissatisfaction and quietly hope things will change on their own. What most people don't realize is that their dissatisfaction is really a message to take action, not sit around in misery. We're not supposed to be happy with less! We live in a universe filled with infinite possibilities, so MORE is always available to us.

That's why we grow so dissatisfied when our relationships aren't growing, our jobs aren't rewarding and our income stays the same. Something in us knows we're supposed to be happy, rich and in love!

You will never get yourself to be happy with less than what you really want from life. You were designed by your Creator to dream great dreams and accomplish wonderful things. Spirit is calling you into a life of greatness—but sometimes (for whatever reason) some of us have to go through the dark before we can find the light.

❧ THE DARK NIGHT OF THE SOUL

"Calls emerge as readily from the ground as from the sky...dark nights of the soul are just as instructive as days of wine and roses, if not more so."

—Gregg Levoy

Sometimes our callings come through the "dark night of the soul" experience—when everything we've tried has failed. When we live completely unconscious to our soul's longing, often times something in our lives has to break "down" before we can have a break "through."

We try to live life by dissecting it into parts and then taking only the parts we like. We love eating the fruit of the tree, but we hate tending to the soil beneath it. We covet the diamond and ignore the pressure it took to create it. We don't want pain. We want pleasure! We don't want questions. We want answers! But answers only come as the questions are asked, and pleasure enters our lives by first listening to what is painful.

The spiritual journey sometimes takes some down-and-dirty work. It calls on us to take a true and realistic view of ourselves and the world we've created around us. When we do this, sometimes we experience sadness or regret. Moving through those feelings will take us to the next step in our growth. Avoiding them will only cause more delays.

Allow the "dark night of the soul" to be a time for "soul listening" and reevaluating choices. It has a great and powerful lesson to teach, IF you will listen.

IN THE TWINKLING OF AN EYE

"It doesn't interest me what you do for a living. I want to know what you ache for, and if you dare to dream of meeting your heart's longing."
—Oriah Mountain Dreamer

Beethoven had a "flash" of inspiration that came to him in one great chord. And in the time it took to snap his finger, he heard an entire symphony. It took him weeks to write it down and today it takes almost an hour for an orchestra to play it. But Beethoven caught it in a flash.

In *Talks with Great Composers*, author Walter Abell quotes Brahms as saying, "I always contemplate my oneness with the Creator before commencing to compose. I immediately feel vibrations that thrill my whole being—straight away the idea flows in upon me—Measure by measure, the finished product is revealed."

We don't have to wait a lifetime for our callings to be revealed. They can come to us in the twinkling of an eye much like they did for Beethoven and Brahms. Sometimes what takes just a minute for the Creator to reveal, takes us a decade to raise the courage to pursue, and the rest of our lives to express.

Don't wait another minute! Spirit is calling—are you listening? Write down the words you hear! Draw what you see! Record the music in your ears! Take the best idea you have, and do something with it! Because if you don't, it will go to someone else who has the courage to pursue it.

❧ How Much Does it Cost?

"Let us take our bloated nothingness out of the path of the divine circuits. Let us unlearn our wisdom of the world. Let us lie low in the Lord's power and learn that truth alone makes us rich and great."

—Ralph Waldo Emerson

Eventually a calling will get your attention, either through inspiration or desperation—or through harmony or disease. That's why we try to avoid or delay them, because we inherently know the price we'll pay for pursuing them.

Spirit is calling us to a greater life—but sometimes we try to ignore the call. We bargain with it. We delay it. We promise it our attention, later. For many of us, we hesitate to pursue our callings until the fear of doing so is finally exceeded by the pain of *not* doing so.

In our quest to be more authentic, we may have to give up: a job, a relationship, prejudice or our need to be right. To rise to a higher good, we have to let go of our "little" selves. By letting go of our lies and rationalizations we find our true, *authentic* selves. The price we pay is well worth the reward of honesty and authenticity.

In his book, *The Universe is Calling*, Eric Butterworth wrote: "There is an upward pull of the universe, ever seeking to lift you to the heights of your divine nature. It is as real and as inexorable as the force of gravity."

Spirit is calling—are you listening? Its only desire is for you to be courageous enough to express who you are. It will not halt until you set yourself free. It will haunt you until you release your true self into the world.

Too many times we seek to separate the good from life—like cream from milk. We only want the "top" layer. And we want to eat as much of it as we desire, without getting fat. We want to grow, but we don't want to change! We want to be rich, but we don't want to give up our poverty thoughts and low self-estimation. These are the fantasies of the spiritually immature.

But, Spirit isn't interested in our childish whining. It pays no attention to our victimizations and powerless careers. It continues to whisper from within: *You are powerful beyond measure! You are more than you are showing!*

Spirit is calling—are you listening? Can you hear the voice of Truth within you—or have you listened to lies so long that you can't tell the difference any more?

A DREAM DEFERRED

"What happens to a dream deferred?
Does it dry up like a raisin in the sun?
Or does it fester like a sore—and then run?
Does it stink like rotten meat?
Or crust and sugar over—Like Syrupy sweet?
Maybe it just sags like a heavy load.
Or does it EXPLODE?"

—Langston Hughes

I used to believe there was a *perfect* time, or a *perfect* place, or a perfect person—so I waited until things were just *perfect* before I took action. Let's just say, I ended up waiting a long time for perfection to come along, and it never showed up. Now I know that the only perfect time is right NOW—and the only perfect place is right HERE—and I AM the perfect person for whom I waited.

Stop waiting for life to change before you take action. Stop waiting for the right time or place. Do what you can, where you are, right now!

THE COURAGE TO BE WHAT SPIRIT MADE YOU TO BE

At some point you must decide whether to be authentic and risk offending someone—or go on pretending to be something you're not—trying not to offend anyone.

There's a part of us that wishes we could have it both ways. On one hand we certainly want to be true to ourselves. But, on the other hand, we want everyone to like us, too.

It's been said that one of the gifts of old age is a stubborn reluctance to be anything but blatantly honest. But, it's not so much a gift of old age as it is an attribute of the spiritually mature.

Know this: You are not here to make the world happy. You are here to be yourself! You are not here to get everyone to like you. You are here to live in a way that allows you to like yourself!

When you finally have the courage to be exactly what Spirit created you to be, in spite of the world's opinion or whether or not it offends other people, then you have found the secret to a happy life.

Ultimately, you must be yourself—because there's just nothing else you'll be very good at!

TO BE, OR NOT TO BE—THAT IS THE QUESTION

"At some stage in life," writes author Richard Geldard, "all thinking beings have to meet the crisis of authority." At some point we all have to decide on whose authority we stand. Will we let out what we have inside, proudly and honorably? Or, will we keep hiding who we are, fearing that we're not good enough? To be, or not to be, that is the question! And it is a question that we have to answer every day.

It is reported that Jesus said, "If you bring forth what is within you, what you bring forth will save you. If you do not bring forth what is within you, what you do not bring forth will destroy you." It is both a promise and a threat.

If we create an authentic life that allows the full expression of Spirit, we tap our inherent potential and are saved from the world's fear and ignorance. But if we do not, then we trap that powerful spiritual energy inside ourselves. And like a pressure cooker left on a high flame, it's just a matter of time before it blows!

What we have inside is far too compelling and too powerful. Eventually we will have to let it loose. It's just a matter of time, really. The question isn't whether we will or will not answer our call. The question is: "When?"

Spirit is calling—are you listening?

ANSWERING THE CALL

By answering the call to live an authentic life, we find out very quickly who supports our honest effort, and who does not. It's one of the reasons why we don't answer more quickly. Because we live in silent fear that those around us aren't going to be quite as supportive as we hoped.

Living an authentic life means resisting the pressure to conform. Sometimes a calling may require you to stand apart from the crowd, or forge an entirely new path. And the crowd gets very upset when one of its members parts company. But those who find the courage to do so, in spite of the pressure of society and the criticism of their peers, will live a life unequaled by their contemporaries.

One such person was the great artist Picasso. On a trip to Spain a few years ago, I took a tour of the Picasso museum in Barcelona. And as I walked down the halls viewing his amazing works, I suddenly realized the immense courage it must have taken to paint as he did. His style was radically different from his peers. His calling was to express in a unique and iconoclastic way—and it must have taken a great deal of courage to listen to and follow that inner urge.

Each one of us has a calling to express our own uniqueness. There is something we can do like no other person alive. God, as an infinite Creator, has given each of us a special gift never before repeated in all of history (a once-in-a-lifetime opportunity). Our happiness and success will come from finding our calling and giving that gift to the world.

When those around you criticize your efforts as strange or peculiar, you may rest assured you're on the right path. Doing what everyone else does, the same way they do it, will get you the same results. An extra-ordinary person has to follow an extra-ordinary agenda. Have faith that what you hear in your heart is right for you. Don't listen to the world. Listen to Spirit in you and you can't go wrong.

⚹ IT LOOKS TOO SCARY

"The idea that is not dangerous is not worthy of being called an idea at all."

—Elbert Hubbard

I heard about a man who had a great vision for the non-profit organization he was leading. And when he shared his ideas in a Board of Director's meeting, everyone was amazed at how grand his vision was for the organization. Several people spoke up saying, *"Well, you've got some pretty lofty goals there Mister—but where will the money come from?"* To which he answered, *"The money will come from wherever it is right now!"*

He knew something they didn't. He knew that money always follows ideas, not the other way around. You start with a vision—and *then,* the money comes. You start by committing yourself to your best idea, even if it scares the hell out of you, and then the resources come to fulfill it.

That's why most people don't pursue their dreams—because they can't see how they would be fulfilled. With the current resources they have, they just can't see how their dream will come into fruition.

Anything that we are truly "called" to do in life will always look scary because it requires us to obtain resources that we don't currently have available. And it calls on us to trust that Spirit will provide those resources at the right and perfect time. True callings insist that we rely upon the Great Invisible (Spirit) as the only source that can fulfill our dreams.

In truth, all of our callings are calls to *faith*. They teach us that we can't get by alone in the world. Without Spirit, we can't find enough in the world to satisfy us. The world's "trinkets" will only amuse us for a short time. Our true and lasting fulfillment can only come through a strong partnership with Spirit—through which, we are meant to dramatically eclipse our current limitations.

⁙ CALL WAITING

"A thrill passes through all men at the reception of new truth, or at the performance of a great action, which comes out of the heart of nature. In these communications the power to see is not separated from the will to do..."

—Ralph Waldo Emerson

What happens to us when we don't pay attention to our callings? What becomes of our lives when we delay the longings we feel inside? Spirit-in-us goes unexpressed!

Author Greg Levoy writes: "Like a child trying to get attention, a symptom will usually get louder and louder over time, the signal coming across with ever-increasing voltage and violence the longer you ignore it." That same truth applies to our callings. When we don't allow Spirit to express what it wants to express in our lives, the call gets louder and louder.

The more we allow Spirit to express in our lives, the greater degree of health, happiness and love we experience. And the less we allow of Spirit's expression, the greater degree of disease, sorrow and "lovelessness" we experience. The key to living a fulfilled life lies in surrendering to Spirit. This act of surrender requires that we let go of our "ego agenda" in favor of THE agenda. To a degree we must say, "Let thy will be done."

Sometimes our calls are layered upon each other. Underneath our calling to "be" lies another calling to "trust." Surrendering our "ego agenda" calls on us to trust that Spirit's agenda will include our higher good as well.

SPIRIT-DRIVEN INSTEAD OF EGO-DRIVEN

Living a life that is Spirit-driven instead of ego-driven is a great challenge. It asks that we trust in things we can't see. It requires us to move forward with our dreams and grand visions, even when we can't see any possibility for their fulfillment. Spirit is always calling on us to trust that what we have inside is significant and valuable. It calls on us to surrender our fears.

When you start to answer this call, suddenly your priorities in life begin to change. Old relationships, careers and desires begin to fall away. You lose interest in ego-pursuits and superficial agendas. You turn away from pretentiousness and prejudice. You develop a greater understanding and compassion for the people around you. It's almost as if you see everything in the world through new eyes—through the eyes of love! Your soul's assignment is being awakened within you.

Poets and mystics have been telling us for centuries to wake up. They have long realized what we so easily forget—that what we have within us can transform our lives. And waking up to it is the first step in our own healing.

The breeze at dawn has secrets to tell you.
Don't go back to sleep.

You must ask for what you really want.
Don't go back to sleep.

People are going back and forth across the doorsill where the
two worlds touch.

The door is round and open.
Don't go back to sleep.

—Rumi

In their book, *The Cultural Creatives*, authors Dr. Paul Ray and Sherry Anderson write about how this awakening affects our lives: "Waking up can be immediately physical, a quiet deep contact between yourself and everything. It can come as the fruit of long practice, leaving you melted and grateful. Waking up can be filled with pain; an ice pick between the shoulder blades or a tearing apart in the soft tissues of the heart. You see how you have harmed someone, or betrayed yourself, or failed to speak out against injustice. You recognize poverty, loneliness, grief that you have resolutely walked past for years, or a lifetime.

Regardless of the content of your experience, when you begin to wake up, you recognize something as genuine. You don't wake up to what is false, but always to what is true at a level you never knew before. Or to what you knew but have forgotten."

This awakening requires you to rethink your life's agenda. It is the first call for change. The second call will come later after you've made changes that bring your life's experience back to authentic living.

CAN YOU HEAR ME NOW?

Too often we tune out the messages Spirit is sending. We subconsciously say: *"I don't want to hear it. Not now. I don't want to be challenged today. I'm not ready to make a change."*

We do this because we don't always want to hear the truth. Inherently, we might know we need to end a marriage, quit a job, or start a new project—but we like to fool ourselves into thinking we can get by without making changes.

We don't want to hear that perhaps we've been selfish or self-centered in our relationships. We don't want to hear that we need to forgive in order to go forward with our lives. We don't want to experience sadness or loss, so we pretend it doesn't exist.

Sometimes we like to pretend it will all go away magically and we won't have to face the challenge to grow and change. Ultimately, we realize that WE are the ones who need to change, not the people we can't get along with. And that's a challenge that sometimes we're up for—but sometimes we're NOT! And that's okay too.

Wisdom is there when you are ready for it. The answers you seek aren't far away. What you need to know to overcome your challenge isn't hiding from you. The better life you dream of is waiting for you, whenever you're ready to change.

BUSY SIGNALS

"If one advances confidently in the direction of his dreams, and endeavors to live the life which he has imagined, he will meet with a success unexpected in common hours."

—Henry David Thoreau, *Walden*

Sometimes we busy our lives with so much activity that our calls aren't able to get through. We can't hear them because we're always on the other line, so to speak. Psychotherapist Eric Maisel suggests that we practice a technique he calls "hushing."

Hushing is what we do when we meditate or listen to our favorite music. It is whatever we do to quiet our minds long enough to get the grocery list of mundane daily activities out of the way. It is a conscious effort to be "open" to Spirit.

Give yourself some "hushing" time every day. Take time out to go within and listen. You will hear a voice inside leading and guiding you toward what's right for you. If you listen closely, it will reveal each and every step necessary to unfold your highest good.

As you listen, be aware that Spirit sometimes communicates things that don't seem logical or sequential. Also know that it will never lead you to do anything harmful to yourself or any other person. All true spiritual messages come directly from love.

Listen courageously! Listen with the intent to *follow*, not lead. Listen, knowing and trusting that Spirit is calling you to release more of the good you hold inside. Allow it to come forth naturally. Don't try to force it or make it happen. Use the following affirmation daily:

> *Spirit-in-me is calling me to a higher purpose.*
> *I am created to live a purposeful life.*
> *I am Spirit's unique way of giving itself to the world.*

❄ CALLING ALL BEINGS

In her book, *Conscious Evolution*, Barbara Marx Hubbard writes at length about the spiritual evolution taking place in a growing number of people today. She calls them the "cultural creatives," and estimates that there are nearly 40 million of them in the United States alone. These people are among the many that are hearing their own personal "callings" and courageously taking action toward them.

She describes how it starts. "It is a feeling within us urging us to be more, to know more, to reach out and touch, to activate our genius, to find our life purpose."

There is a "spiritual pattern" at the center of who we are. It is Spirit's signature on our lives. Within it lies the full picture of what we are to be. In other words, "something-in-us" already knows what our calling is and how to fulfill it. So, we don't have to figure it out for ourselves. It's already known in Mind!

Spirit is calling YOU—and it will continue to call until you answer! It knows what you are capable of accomplishing. It knows your talent. It knows what you were "made" to do. It knows your likes and dislikes.

Spirit does not make mistakes. Your calling has been perfectly designed. It is matched specifically to your talent. It is the only thing you can do that will "complete" you—and it is the only thing you can do with genius.

Allow the calling to emerge from within you. Trust Spirit to provide the ways and means for it to become a reality. Learn to depend on what you have *within* you and everything *around* you will be transformed to match your dream.

✳ CLAIM YOUR GOOD AND TAKE YOUR RIGHTFUL PLACE WITH SPIRIT

The spiritually aware are rising up in the world with a new vision of possibility. They are waking up to their unlimited potential as spiritual beings. Millions of people are hearing the call from within: Rise up and know that ye are Gods!

Of course, we are not all that God is—yet all that we are is God—like a wave to the ocean. We are created in the image and likeness of God. We share the same Spirit. We are ONE! And this heritage brings with it certain rights and responsibilities.

Our first responsibility is to ourselves. We are first called to be our authentic selves—to be honest about who we are, to know the power we possess, and to use that power constructively, not destructively.

Our second responsibility is to our fellow beings. Our second calling is for understanding and compassion of the human condition. Our responsibility to them is to provide an example of an empowered life, and to lift them up wherever possible.

And finally, our third responsibility is to the world. Our final calling is to leave the world a better place than we found it. We do this by taking action in the world based on our newly awakened spiritual power.

Wake up! It's time to take your rightful place in the universe. It's time for you to use your power. It's time for you to give your gift!

❧ YOU ARE THE LIGHT OF THE WORLD

"From within or from behind, a light shines through us upon things and makes us aware that we are nothing, but the light is all."
—Ralph Waldo Emerson, *The Oversoul*

What you have *within* you is always greater than anything going on around you. What you have *within* you has the power to overcome any obstacle and heal any disease. You were created as an inlet and an outlet for Spirit's expression. You were designed as an opportunity for good.

Trust your calling. It is right for you! And whatever needs to take place for it to come into fruition will take place. If all hell has to break loose, then it will. All obstacles will be removed and the road ahead will be leveled—awaiting your arrival. Nothing will stand in your way while pursuing your calling, if you are in true partnership with Spirit.

Good wants to happen. Spirit wants to be expressed through you. Your calling awaits your faithful attention. Do you have the courage to pursue it?

Spirit is calling—are you listening?

CHAPTER SIX

Spiritual Growth

ACCEPTING THINGS AS THEY ARE

As spiritual beings living a human experience, we share two things in common with every person alive. First of all, we share our Divine potential—that inherent power that allows us to rise above any condition and circumstance. And secondly, we share our human pain—the disappointments and losses that occur in every human life.

Since we share these two commonalities with every person, we tend to bond with others by associating with one or the other. Either we are drawn to each other to achieve some great purpose—to express our Divine potential—or we come together to share our common pain.

Both ways are valid and can be healing. By sharing our pain with another person, we build the strength to overcome it. We learn that everyone has had painful experiences in life. No one escapes the human experience without pain. Ironically, it is a *necessary* part of our lives on planet earth.

Pain is Necessary, Suffering is Optional

Without pain we wouldn't learn what action or which direction is *wrong* for us to pursue. Pain is a "guidance system" that helps us know what NOT to do. We experience pain in life when something's wrong. It is life's signal for us to pay close attention to what we're doing. For instance, if a relationship becomes painful or hurtful, love is no longer present. If it's painful to get up and go to work each day, you're in the wrong profession. Pain is necessary as an information system that guides us away from what isn't right for us.

However, suffering is not necessary. Suffering is what happens when we don't stop doing what's painful! When we don't get out of a bad relationship that causes us pain, we start to suffer. When we don't give healing attention to physical pain, we begin to suffer. Suffering happens because we don't *listen* to pain!

The good news is: We don't have to suffer. It was never part of the Divine plan. We can learn to stop doing what's painful and avoid suffering altogether.

We suffer today because we continue to call into today's experience past events that were painful. We suffer through them again and again, even though the actual pain we felt at impact could have been over and done with a long time ago.

Many people carry the pain they felt from past events into their daily lives. So they have condemned themselves to repeat the same negative experiences over and over again—suffering through them each time.

The way to get off the "suffering merry-go-round" is to find a way to accept things as they are. We can release pain and move on with life only through forgiveness and acceptance. And it is much easier to accept things as they are by remembering three basic truths:

1. People are always doing their very best.
2. Every person's intention was to do good.
3. At the core of our being, we are ALL inherently good.

People Are Always Doing Their Very Best

As a rule, when we learn how to improve something we're doing and make it more successful, we immediately incorporate that wisdom into our lives. When we learn to do something better, we immediately become more proficient at it. We don't ignore what we learned and continue unsuccessfully. We assimilate the better technique and become more effective at what we're trying to accomplish. Raising multiple children is a good example of this truth. The techniques parents develop in raising their first child they apply to the second and third, refining them as they go along. They take what they know and use it more effectively.

This same truth applies to everything we do. We are always operating at peak capacity with the wisdom we currently possess. We are always doing the very best we can with the information we have at the time. Learning to accept yourself as you are and other people as they are begins by knowing this truth.

Every Person's Intention Was to Do Good

No one sets out to screw up their life, or the lives of the people around them. We don't *intend* to hurt people or create havoc. Everyone's intentions are honorable and forthright. We set out to experience love and joy. We just don't always know how.

Of course, this doesn't excuse people's negative behavior or rationalize their abuse. It is merely a statement of truth that will help you heal and forgive. Whoever they are and whatever they did to hurt you—they did not maliciously intend to harm you. They were acting out their own abuse and reacting to their own pain and hurt. And although it may *appear* they meant to cause you harm, on a soul-to-soul level their intentions were honorable.

At the core of our being, we are ALL inherently good.

Every person on earth was created by the same Spirit. Each of us possesses the same Life Force within us. No matter what behavior we display on the outside, within us lies a perfect Spirit waiting and wanting to be revealed. Inside every soul is a perfect Divine seed.

But as perfect and wonderful as that seed may be, it cannot grow without our own permission and acknowledgement of it. Like the seeds of a plant can only grow in soil when they are given the correct balance of water and sunlight, the Divine-seed within us needs our own loving care and attention to grow. We cannot fully realize our innate potential without a spiritual awakening to its presence.

So, although at the core of our being we may all be perfect and good, only those who recognize their soul's assignment to let out the love we have inside become a blessing to the world. Others will have to wait until they are worn down by the repetitiousness of negativity until they awaken to their soul's purpose.

When You KNOW Better, You Will DO Better!

"Until we know correctly we cannot do right, live well, or become greater than we are. We cannot make our lives or our world better by trying not to do something we have the urge to do, but only by knowing that there is something better to do and that we can find a way to do it."
—Dr. Kennedy Shultz, *You Are The Power*

Every attempt to manipulate human behavior has failed. Telling people what they *shouldn't* be doing is an exercise in futility.

People who are overweight know they *should* change their diet and exercise. People who are living unhealthy lifestyles know they *should* change their habits. And sometimes at the beginning of a new year or the anniversary of a special event, they will *try* to get themselves to change. But usually the change doesn't last very long—and then they feel the shame of yet another failed attempt.

You can't put the cart before the horse. You can't change your behavior before you change your awareness. But if you change your awareness first, then your behavior will change automatically. Virtue is inherent, and right action is natural. People don't set themselves up to fail; but they can only act from what wisdom they currently possess. So, the key to a more successful life isn't to *do* better, it's to *know* better.

Stop trying to get yourself to behave or to conform to some identity that others say you *should* have. Remember that you are a "response-able" person *choosing* how to respond to life. Don't allow someone else to choose for you! Reexamine your past responses and evaluate their success. Have they given you the kind of life experience you want? Have they empowered and uplifted you? Did they make you feel more confident, or more fearful? What changes can you make? Trust that as you know better, you will automatically do better!

THE WAY YOU SEE THE PROBLEM, IS THE PROBLEM

Because of our distorted perception, the problems and limitations in our lives seem astronomical, while the power to overcome them seems insignificant. This is why most people rarely succeed beyond the average experience of life—because they don't realize the true reality of their circumstances.

The truth is: Our problems, challenges and limitations are tiny, little, insignificant matters compared with the immense power we have to overcome them. WE ARE POWERFUL BEINGS!

All of our power is generated from within. It rises up from within to meet whatever challenge it is faced with. This power is "spiritual power" that comes directly from the life of God within every individual. And it is limitless. That's why somehow we always have just enough strength or wisdom to meet our challenge. Even though we doubt we've got what it takes to make it through our challenge, something *in* us always rises to the surface to give us strength.

When we withdraw all of the negative energy that we contribute to the problem by worrying over it, we gather the wisdom and power to survive it—and with our new survival skills there comes a renewed sense of confidence. We're not responsible for solving problems. We don't have to figure out how to heal our bodies or attract the perfect mate. That's not our job in life. That's God's job!

Give it up! Let go of the problem. Release the tight-hold grip you have on it and surrender it to the spiritual Power that created the universe. And then watch what happens. If you really let it go and resist trying to snatch it back in a fit of panic, you'll see that everything will work out for the best. You really can trust God to know exactly what to do to bring about the highest good for all.

Stop *looking* at the problem. Stop *talking* about the problem. It's really not that interesting. Stop worrying about the problem. Go within and say: "*God, You know the way out of this mess, so show me. You have the power and resources to heal it. I don't. So, from now on, I'm leaving it all up to you. Show me what's mine to do—and I'll do it. But whatever else there is to do, I trust you to take care of it.*"

❧ TAKE A LESSON FROM NATURE

I attended a dog show a few years ago and was stunned at the incredible variety in this one species. There were big, muscular looking animals and small, frail ones. Some of them pranced around like models and others clomped around looking goofy. And it made me stop and think about the amazing variety in every species on our planet.

It seems to me that either our Creator has an incredible sense of humor, an affection for the ridiculous—or just a simple need to express itself in a wide variety of forms. The very fact that we have millions of different life forms in our world speaks volumes. Perhaps the nature of Nature is to keep inventing and arranging new expressions of life—none of which are quite alike.

And yet somehow it all seems to work together! The plants release oxygen and humans inhale it. One life form provides sustenance for another. What one species lacks, another has in abundance. The wild fires destroy the forest one season and new growth arises from the ashes in the next. For every death, there is a birth. For every loss, there is a gain, for every defect, an asset. Nature *balances* herself in perfect precision!

Perhaps we can learn a lesson from nature that will help us understand the challenges we face and why we have to go through them. Perhaps for everything "bad" that happens, we are compensated with something "good."

For Every Loss There Is a Gain

"Nature hates monopolies and exceptions. Every excess causes a defect; every defect an excess. Every sweet hath its sour; every evil its good. For every grain of wit there is a grain of folly. For everything you have missed, you have gained something else; and for everything you gain, you lose something."

—Ralph Waldo Emerson, *Compensation*

Since it is the nature of Nature to seek balance, a loss in one area is always compensated by a gain in another. Given the perspective of hindsight, and the healing power of *time,* this truth will ultimately reveal itself in our own lives as well.

But at the first moment of loss, it's easy to forget. Initially, our loss seems *personal* and *cruel.* It seems unjust and uncaring. We look up at the sky and shout angrily at our God, *"How could you? What good could possibly be served in this tragedy?"*

But over time, we learn to accept our loss and to integrate it into our life's experience. Instead of leaving a gaping hole in our hearts, the wound comes together to create some new experience for us, the same way a scab forms when we cut our skin. This new experience is the compensation we are to gain for our loss.

Talk to anyone who's faced a "serious" illness and come through it to the other side healed, and they'll tell you their experience caused them to reevaluate their priorities. It called on them to push the reset button and realign themselves with a new purpose and new vision for being alive.

Ask any widow and they'll tell you that after a proper mourning period they were able to find new strengths and talents that had gone undiscovered in their previous life. For everything we lose, we gain something new! Nature "compensates" every loss in an attempt to restore balance and order to our lives.

In truth, there is no loss without a gain. For everything we lose, we gain something else. If we lose our sight, our hearing becomes clearer. If we lose our job, we learn that our value doesn't come from our employer. If we lose a spouse, the direction of our lives changes course and with that comes new opportunities. Look for the "compensation" and you will find it.

"Order comes out of disorder, form out of chaos, as it did in the creation of the universe."

—Rollo May

WHERE THERE IS CONFLICT, THERE IS GROWTH

I saw Barbra Streisand interviewed on television a few years ago. And she was talking about how emotionally unavailable her father was—and how she used to sing and dance for him as a little girl to gain his attention and approval. Then the interviewer asked, *"Do you think you would have pursued a career as an entertainer had it not been for your father's emotional inabilities?"* And her answer was astounding. She said, *"No, I don't believe I would have."*

Very often in life, the thing we think is the *worst* that could happen, ends up being the very motivation we need to get ahead. Sometimes the thing we struggle with and curse is exactly the same thing trying to move us forward.

In his essay "Circles," Emerson writes: "People wish to be settled: only as far as they are unsettled is there any hope for them..." We may not like the uncomfortableness of change, but it is necessary for our growth. Where there is friction and challenge in our lives, there is something of value wanting to be received.

Every story has an antagonist. Every person serves as some kind of example for us. Every experience we've had, whether we call it negative or positive, has something of value to bring to our lives. Sometimes, the very thing we struggle with is where our calling lies. The mythologist Joseph Campbell once said, "Where you stumble, there is your treasure."

Very likely, the thing you've been praying for is right under your nose. So, if you stumble, don't get up and curse the ground. Look around. There might be a treasure right where you fell!

And if you're still blaming your parents, like Streisand once did, for what they didn't have to give you—take another look and see how their character (or lack of character) might have contributed something good to your life. If there is something good there for you to receive—take it and move on.

❊ Meeting Your Creator

Human life is a process of discovery. Every experience we encounter or create shows us some truth about ourselves. We are not here to learn lessons per se. We are here to unfold the truth of what we are—to discover that God has placed itself inside each of us in a unique pattern. God is not an "external" event. It is an "internal" awareness!

That's why the prophet Paul told us that we would be transformed by the renewing of our own *minds*. He didn't say that transformation would come from a person, or a location. It's an "inner" experience that comes as a result of knowing the God within you.

Many people have been taught to *fear* God. Some have wondered whether there really is a God. Others go through life without pursuing any spiritual connection at all. Few people really *know* God, or have any *personal* relationship with Spirit. But those who do lead lives that are very different from the rest. They are the ones who are truly transformed.

All of our experiences, challenges, dramas and traumas in life are designed to bring us face to face with God. They are inroads to the Divine—opportunities to reveal what has been hidden inside. And perhaps it's human nature to want to curse them as we go through them. But when we get to the other side of our challenge, feeling triumphant and courageous for having slayed the dragon we faced, then our perspective changes. Now we see our challenges for the Divine events they really were.

How do you know you're truly courageous until you've faced the thing that scares the hell out of you? How do you know the limit of your patience unless someone you know has worked your last nerve? How will you know the depth of forgiveness unless you are called upon to forgive the "unforgivable?"

Every challenge we face brings us closer to the strength and power we've always had inside. They are calls to the Divine to rise up within us—so that we can *know* and *feel* the presence of God. They are appointments with our soul's destiny to be a co-creator with Spirit.

CHAPTER SEVEN

Living the Dream: Co-Creation

 CONSCIOUS CO-CREATORS

*Conscious evolution inspires in us a mysterious and humble
awareness that we have been created by this awesome process of
evolution and are now being transformed by it to take a more
mature role as co-creators. In this view we do not stand apart from
nature, but, rather, we are nature evolving.*

—Barbara Marx Hubbard, *Conscious Evolution*

For thousands of years the human race has seen itself as
victims in an unfriendly universe. We believed we were part of
some mysterious plan that we could neither understand, nor control. We perceived ourselves as pawns in a war between powers for
good and evil. At one point in our history, we even believed we
were alive just to provide amusement for the gods. The question
as to *why* we are here has crossed the mind of every man and
woman since the beginning of time. And now, the answer to that

question is finally being revealed!

We have matured spiritually beyond victimization. We are coming to see ourselves in a whole new light. We now understand our true role in life is to become a *co-creator.* Nature has spent fifteen billion years evolving human consciousness so that we could assume full partnership in the creative process. In other words, God didn't create pawns, it made *partners!*

We were designed to interact with Spirit—not to be a victim of random forces. Finally, as maturing co-creators we're beginning to see our grown-up responsibilities. In the past, we've used our creative abilities destructively. For centuries we've lived in fear of each other, building up cultures just to tear them down again. Many great civilizations have come and gone. Even today in the 21st century, we still resist these old self-destructive tendencies to create—and then destroy what we've created.

But we *will* resist them—and learn to use our power only for constructive means. Inevitably, the human race will reveal the greatness it has within it. We have been designed by our Creator to succeed. Nature didn't go to all of this trouble just to see us fail. The intelligence at the helm in the universe knows exactly what it is doing.

Every time you think, you interact with this intelligence. Each thought you choose to entertain becomes a new creation. The way you use your mind not only determines the quality of *your* life experience, it also makes an impression in the world.

God created each of us as full partners in the creative process, so we have a responsibility to leave a positive impact on future generations of co-creators by using our power affirmatively.

Start today by seeing yourself in full partnership with Spirit to co-create your life. Think of yourself as a powerful being in a "user-friendly" universe. Remember that God is always on the side of *good.* So, think good thoughts. Think about what or whom you love. Think about what you really want to see happen in your life and in our world. Dare to dream BIG dreams!

The greatest contribution you can make to this world is a life well-lived! The world doesn't need another unhappy soul, nor does it need another victim. It needs you to wake up and take your position as a spiritually mature, conscious, co-creator with God— whose primary responsibility is to bring something *good* to life.

Living in Partnership with a Higher Power

Contrary to popular belief, we are not victims in life, or random accidents of nature. We are powerful co-creators designed to be interactive with our Creator! Life doesn't happen to us. It happens through us. We're involved in an eternal partnership with God—the one Creative Power in the universe. And we each have been given a full partnership in life. No one has less status or more talent. We are all equals.

To take your position as a partner with this loving power you must be clear on what your responsibility is and what your partner's responsibility is. Two partners work best together when each one is allowed to do what they do best.

Your role in the partnership is to:

- Be an open channel to receive new ideas.
- Create space and time in your life to listen to the ideas passing through your mind.
- Pay attention to gentle urgings and reoccurring themes.
- Sift through your greatest ideas and see which ones have the most appeal. (An infinite mind has infinite possibilities. You won't receive just *one* dream. You will have many choices. Try each one on, like a new shirt or blouse, to see if it fits.)
- Listen to your heart's desire. The intellect may lead you

around in circles, but the heart always knows what's real.
- Make a decision as to what you want—and stick to it. Never give up! When the dream is right, no matter what obstacles appear, they can and will be overcome.

Emerson said that God will not have His work made manifest by cowards. So your primary responsibility will always be to maintain trust and courage. Living in partnership with Spirit may require you to step out in faith, not knowing exactly how your dream will be manifest. Like Indiana Jones, at some point you won't be able to see the path beneath your feet. But it is always there. Spirit won't take you down any path that will cause you harm.

Spirit's role in the partnership is:
- To gather whatever resources are necessary to fulfill your dream and place them on your path.
- To have the dream bring equal or greater value to your life as well as others. (In other words, it's supposed to make you rich!)
- To make its presence known to you.

As you pursue your dreams, remain open and flexible. God has many resources that you're not aware of. And Spirit has its own timing, which may or may not be convenient for you. In the end you will know *why* everything happened as it did.

Guidelines to Remember When Co-Creating

- You are not here to *learn*—you are here to *live!*
- You are not here to *evolve*—you are here to *emerge!*
- You are not here to *get* the best—you are here to *give* the best!
- You are not here to *win*—you are here to have a *spiritual experience!*

• You are not here to *get* your way—you are here to *find* your way!

As partners with Spirit we co-create every part of our lives including career, finances, personal relationships, and even our own health.

CO-CREATING CAREER

"There is a tendency to deal with our work-life almost as if it were a life sentence from which we may ultimately retire as time off for good behavior."

—Eric Butterworth, *Spiritual Economics*

Your workplace doesn't have to be a house of ill repute where you prostitute yourself daily just to have money to pay your bills. Nor is it a prison, confining you to a certain cubicle with an iron ball and chain. The word "vocation" comes from the Latin, meaning, "I call." Your work is your *calling*. It should be matched with the unique talent that Spirit gave you.

Everyone has been given a special talent that no other person on the planet may possess. Even people in the same profession with the same title have different talents and ways in which to approach their success. And one profession isn't better than another. Spirit doesn't value accountants more than waitresses. We all hold equal status in the eyes of God so it doesn't matter what career we choose. What matters is that it brings us a sense of joy and self-fulfillment.

If you're working just for money, you'll never find true happiness or prosperity. You're not here to make a living; you're here to make a life! Success isn't measured by acquiring things. It's measured by giving who you are to the world. We're not here to get lots of "stuff." We're here to recognize the value we have to give—and then give it!

We are never a success because of what we *have*. We are always a success because of what we are. Whatever toys we obtain in the process are strictly for our own amusement—just as children's toys are for their amusement. They are to be played with, enjoyed, and then thrown away to make way for new ones.

No matter what your job, your true business is the *express* business. You are here to release your imprisoned splendor. You are here to BE! You are here to discover your unique talent and then give it to the world. In doing this, you will find your true career and end up living very prosperously. Eric Butterworth tells us to "remember that consciousness is the key. Make a new commitment to think of your work not as a place to make a living, but as an opportunity to make a life."

Stop looking for a job and start looking *within* for your true calling. Think of what you were *born* to do—and then seek an employment outlet that matches your calling. Decide what you want to do and then call upon the infinite resources of God to create the perfect outlet for that talent.

Points to Remember:

- Your work is your "calling."
- God does not value accountants more than waitresses. It doesn't care what you do with your talent—as long as it brings you joy and fulfillment.
- You don't succeed when you have lots of "stuff." You succeed by being who you are—and giving your unique self to your work.

OLD WORK ETHIC

1. Children play, grownups *work*. Work is what officially makes you grown up.
2. Work is something you have to go looking for "out there" in the world. You apply for it and compete for it.
3. Work is what fathers go away in the morning to do all day. It is very serious and somewhat mysterious because it happens far away—at someplace called the office or the plant. Most mothers work at home, but that doesn't count as *real* work.
4. Work is not something you're supposed to like.
5. People who don't work are either very poor or very rich. Poor people who don't work are lazy and contemptible.
6. Losing your job is one of the most shameful and terrible things that can happen.

SPIRITUAL WORK ETHIC

1. Work is an area of great passion. It is an opportunity for self-expression.
2. Work is our particular "calling." It fulfills our desire to contribute something good to the world.
3. Work is an enjoyable experience. It's fun!
4. Every job is equally important because it fulfills the individual doing it. Women and men are equal partners in the work place.
5. Changing jobs is nothing more than an opportunity for growth and change. There is no shame in it.
6. There is no competition. Each person contributes something unique.

CO-CREATING ABUNDANCE
Balance Your Books

"...it is your Father's good pleasure to give you the kingdom."
—*The Bible*

Nature maintains wholeness through circulation. Water must circulate to remain fresh. Blood must flow through our veins to sustain health. The wind must blow so that the air doesn't become rancid. Everything in nature is in a constant state of circulation.

That same truth must be applied to our financial lives. It is impossible to live an abundant life if you are always worrying about money. You must have a constantly increasing flow of money into your life to continue living well.

The good news is: That's exactly what Spirit has in mind for you. God created you to live well and prosper! You were designed by a limitless life to live in the lap of luxury. And not only is it your *right* to prosper, it is also your *duty*. Because in doing so, you reveal the true nature of God. By living a prosperous life, you provide the world with an example of a life lived in communion with Spirit.

Although some religions have trouble reconciling their doctrines with prosperous living, true spirituality is based on an intimate, personal relationship with Spirit. Not a limited, angry old man-in-the-sky God—but God as an unlimited Provider of all good things.

The nature of this inexhaustible, unlimited Being is to GIVE! It takes great pleasure in sharing all that it has. And we were created to receive this Divine outpouring of good. In other words, we are heirs to the entire estate!

Your Fortune Begins With You

"God can do no more for you than He can do through you. All the help of God cannot aid you except as it flows through your consciousness, through your faith, through your vision. So before you attempt to raise money, the first step should be to raise consciousness..."

—Eric Butterworth

Any attempt to live life from the outside—in is fruitless. We must first change our *inner* thoughts—and then the *outer* experience will automatically reflect those changes. A change in consciousness is always a prerequisite to increased prosperity. Without it, you are just "fund-raising." And any increase in funds will automatically be wasted or lost without the consciousness to support it.

The rich get richer and the poor get poorer—and not because it is a cruel act of an unloving god. They continue to repeat the same experience in their lives because they maintain the same state of consciousness in their minds. They have formed a *belief system* that supports their experience of wealth or poverty.

The *rich* are thinking about:

• How much good they have in their lives
• How happy they are to have it
• How they can use it to produce more

The *poor* are thinking about:

• How little good they have in their lives
• How unfair it is that they don't have more
•How fearful they are that there won't be enough

True and lasting wealth is automatically drawn to those who believe:
- There is an unlimited, eternal supply of good
- They are worthy of prosperity
- Their self-value comes from Spirit
- It is God's INTENTION for them to prosper
- You can't afford to hold on to resentments—they limit the flow of good into YOUR life.
- Nothing is "too good" for me!
- Every day is a new opportunity to prosper
- Good can come from anywhere, at anytime
- Lack of funds is a temporary experience that cannot last

Check Your Attitude

What is your attitude toward money? Do you avoid thinking about it? Or do you obsess over every penny spent?

Many people avoid dealing with money issues until they're faced with some financial crisis. They don't balance their checkbooks regularly, are unaware of how much they owe and don't understand money issues. They delay saving until they hit middle age and then panic when they realize they won't have enough to retire. Denial and avoidance are common practices when it comes to dealing with their money issues.

If you want to live a more prosperous life, learn about money. Educate yourself. Read magazines and books. Take a money-management course from the local college or an investment course from one of the large brokerage houses. Many are offered free of charge. Talk to a certified financial planner or a friend who handles money well. Don't be embarrassed or afraid to ask questions. Everyone has to learn for themselves how to deal with money—and it's not an issue that most people were well educated about.

The Best Formula for Using Your Money

Like everything else that's good in life, money requires us to use it responsibly and with wisdom. As a teacher of prosperity and a truly prosperous person myself, here is the formula I have found works best with money:

1. Give some.
2. Save some.
3. Spend some.

Use your money according to this formula (and in this order) and you will always have more than enough.

When you receive any monies, take ten percent off the top and GIVE IT AWAY *first!* Give it to any person, company or organization that will use your money to uplift the world. Give it to your church. Give it to a non-profit center that is working to relieve suffering in third-world countries. Give it to any cause that you really believe in, and want to support. By giving your money away *first,* you are acknowledging it as a circulating flow—and trusting in the source of your supply (Spirit/God). It is an act of faith that is always rewarded when given in love and joy.

Secondly, take at least another ten percent and put it into a savings plan. Create an IRA or buy stocks, bonds or mutual funds. Perhaps you might want to open a savings account at a local bank. (If you decide to do so, do not order an ATM card on the account. It will be too tempting to use.) After you acknowledge your source (Spirit) by giving some of your money away, pay yourself next. Save some of your money so that each time you receive the monthly asset-statement you will begin to see yourself grow in prosperity. This helps to create a consciousness of worth and value and is a very important step in building permanent wealth.

You are not saving for a "rainy day." You are saving to create and support a consciousness of wealth. Early withdrawals are not allowed except to invest in something that will provide greater returns such as real estate or a new business venture.

And last, but not least, take the eighty percent you have left and spend it on products and services that you value. ONLY buy what you love and are proud to own! Don't spend your money frivolously, or on things that you will complain about owning later. In building a consciousness of prosperity, it is very important to spend your money consciously.

If you are in debt, find out how much and to whom. Don't live in the dark, not knowing how much you owe. You can't afford to have uncertainty about money. Create a monthly plan to get yourself out of debt and vow to stop using all credit cards immediately. Balance your books and you will begin to balance your life!

Creating a Healthy Relationship with Money

Like any personal relationship with a loved one or family member, your relationship with money is built over time. Learn to *trust* yourself with money.

I once had a friend who would only take $20.00 out of her account at a time because she was afraid if she took more, she'd spend it. So, I said to her, *"What you're really saying when you do that is that you don't trust yourself with your own money!"*

Take a larger amount out of the ATM machine than you normally would and use it less frequently. Practice what it feels like to have money in your pocket without having to spend it all immediately. Watch yourself save money. Feel the feelings of increase and supply. Allow yourself to prosper. When others offer to pay, let them.

Stop devaluing your talent. When you provide a service or product, ask for a fee. Work with people who value what you offer and don't work with others who continue to question your worth. Resist short-term rewards such as using your money to shift your mood. When you're in a sad or angry mood—do NOT spend money. Give and spend money only out of a sense of love and joy.

Going through the process of restoring financial health and learning new skills around money is a long-term commitment. By doing both the inner and outer work, you are setting a strong foundation for a healthy relationship with money. Live long and prosper!

⚘ CO-CREATING LOVE AND FRIENDSHIP

"My friends have come to me unsought. The great God gave them to me."
—Ralph Waldo Emerson

According to an old Sufi tale, one afternoon Nasruddin and his friend were sitting in a café drinking tea and talking about love and relationships.

"How come you never got married, Nasruddin?" asked his friend. "Well," said Nasruddin, "to tell you the truth, I spent my youth looking for the perfect woman. In Cairo, I met a beautiful and intelligent woman, with eyes like dark olives, but she was unkind. Then in Baghdad, I met a woman who was a wonderful and generous soul, but we had no interests in common. One woman after another would seem just right, but there would always be something missing. Then one day, I met her. She was beautiful, intelligent, generous and kind. We had everything in common. In fact, she was perfect!"

"Well," said Nasruddin's friend, "What happened? Why didn't you marry her?" Nasruddin sipped his tea reflectively, "Well," he replied, "It's a sad thing. It seems that she was looking for the perfect man."

Just like Nasruddin, we're always trying to find perfection *outside* ourselves. We think of love as something some other person has, that we lack. And if we can convince them to give it to us, then we'll be valuable and worthwhile. Yet, the truth is: Love isn't something you *get*. It's something you *give!*

As a co-creator with God, it's important to understand and cooperate with spiritual law. One of the most basic spiritual law states: "What you send out, must return back to you." So, if you want love and friendship in your life, then you must "send out" love. This law ensures that every person can only receive what they are first willing to *give.*

If you're seeking to demonstrate greater love or friendship in your life, begin by *giving* love. Start by giving love to every person you meet. Be a friend to the people around you. If you'll do this, two hearts will connect and friendships will be formed. Love *wants* to happen, so Spirit is always trying to put people together who have the capacity to love one another.

We seek each other's company because God-in-us knows that what we can be *together* far exceeds what we can be apart. That's the principle behind the statement: "Where two or more are gathered, there shall I be."

Love is a unique and powerful force in the universe. It breaks all boundaries and overcomes every prejudice. It has its own sequence and time. It cannot be scheduled or manipulated.

Friendships and loving relationships are always Divinely ordained. Nothing can force them into being. They can only come about through the interaction of consciousness. So, create a consciousness that is a magnet to love by giving love on every occasion.

The answers to life's questions are always simple. Love is not a difficult thing to demonstrate in one's life. It's simply a matter of building a consciousness of love—each day working to realize the value of your own unique contribution.

Be sure you are "sending out" only what you want to receive back. If you are seeking honesty in your relationships, are *you* being honest? If you are seeking financial stability, are *you* financially stable? Give what you want to receive!

Points to Remember:

- What you send out must return back to you. It's a spiritual law.
- Just because you *want* more, doesn't mean you'll *get* more. You have to GIVE the very thing you want to receive.
- We are drawn together by nature—because what we can be *together* far exceeds what any of us can apart. We are one human family. We belong together.

Co-Creating Health
Dying on Cue

A lot of my friends were dying in the 1980's because that's what the doctors told them to do. In the early discovery years of HIV, doctors believed that patients who acquired the virus had approximately six months to live.

So, one of my friends went to the doctor for the HIV test only to find out he tested positive. The doctor suggested that he get his "affairs in order" and prepare to live about another six months. And that's exactly what he did. He died on cue within six months!

Later, it was determined that the HIV virus is quite elusive. It can actually lie dormant in the human body for up to twenty years without activating. And it made me think of my friend who died within six months. Did he die because he had AIDS, or because that's what he believed he had to do? He was in perfect health before he found out he was HIV positive—but then six months later he was in a casket. Was it the *disease* that killed him, or was he literally scared to death?

Norman Cousins said that, "The greatest force in the human body is the natural drive of the body to heal itself—but that force is not independent of the belief system, which can translate expectations into physiological change. Nothing is more wondrous about the 15 billion neurons in the human brain than their ability to convert thoughts, hopes, ideas and attitudes into chemical substances. Everything begins, therefore, with belief. What we believe is the most powerful option of all."

Every thought creates a chemical reaction in your body. Every emotion causes some condition in the body. Science has proved that people who have the support system of a spiritual community tend to be healthier and live longer. Also, married couples and people who have partners tend to be healthier than their single counterparts.

Clearly, we are already co-creators in our own health simply by the lifestyle choices we make each day. We can't control every germ or plan every event. But we can stand at the doorway of our belief, only allowing in thoughts that are life-affirming.

There is no real mind/body connection because there's nothing to connect. They are already ONE! Your thoughts and feelings translate into physicality. They are either creating the conditions in your body that support health, or they are defeating your body's natural immune responses, thereby leaving you open to disease. In other words: What you think about your health may be the single most important factor in determining whether you're healthy or not!

It is a well-known fact that a new drug is most effective in healing when it is first released on the market. Over time, slowly, the new drug becomes less effective. This is believed to be so because the public's expectations are high when a new drug is first released. They have *faith* that it will work. But then, their faith fades and so does the effectiveness of the drug.

This phenomenon tells us that our belief seems to be just as important as the actual chemical in the drug. This could be another demonstration of the power of the mind to heal or to destroy the body, like my friend who died on cue for his doctor.

Health is Normal

"Be ye therefore perfect, even as your Father which is in heaven is perfect."
                                                            —The Bible

Health is our normal and natural state of being. It's the way our bodies are designed to be. The intelligence within them (Spirit) is always at work seeking to maintain health. Unbeknownst to us, billions of interactions are taking place every minute within our bodies, bringing together resources we haven't yet discovered to sustain our health. It is the nature of our bodies to be healthy.

Some people believe that within the physical body there is a *spiritual* body that is always perfect. That spiritual body has never been affected by any pain or disease of the flesh. It is our *true* self, free from the limitations of physicality. The spiritual body lives in and through the physical body. It does not age or change. It is always healthy. In other words, the physical body may experience disease—but the spiritual body is always in perfect shape.

Disease is not our true nature. We were not designed by our Creator to live in sickness. We were created for health. We know that health is our true and natural state because it is what we return to, though we may experience periods of illness. Disease is *episodic*. But health is permanent. Wholeness is the normal state of our spiritual body. When the physical body can no longer sustain itself, the spiritual body separates from it and returns back to its source. Physical death is also a *natural* process.

We are not designed to stay in our physical bodies forever. They are temporary vehicles designed specifically for a short-term journey. This does not mean, however, that in order to make an exit, you have to get sick. Many people die simply because they are ready—not because they have fallen victim to some ridiculous disease.

Disease Has No Agenda for Your Life

In 1985, I was in my favorite dry cleaners waiting for the guy behind the counter to gather up my clothes. The employee was rather flamboyant and obviously gay. He was a friendly man who always had something positive to say.

As I was standing there talking to him at the counter, a frustrated woman came in complaining that a spot didn't come out of a blouse she had picked up the day before. As she handed the blouse back to the man behind the counter, he apologized and said he would do his best to get the spot out.

But "doing his best" wasn't good enough for her. She demanded he take care of it immediately! Once again, the man apologized—but then explained that she wasn't the only customer needing care, as he pointed to thousands of garments on the line just behind him.

She became belligerent and grabbed her blouse off the counter and scurried to the door. Just as she was about to exit, she turned, looked him straight in the eyes and said, "I hope all of you gay people die of AIDS!"

In the 1980's some people, who called themselves Christian, believed that the AIDS epidemic was sent by God to kill off those "immoral" homosexuals. Not only is this a shocking conclusion, it's also quite ignorant.

It's hard for me to believe in a God who would use such a horrible atrocity for any good purpose. What kind of God would use disease as a means to bring anything good to people's lives? What agenda or purpose could it have?

I don't believe disease comes from God. We don't need to get sick in order to appreciate good health, anymore than we need to be choked in order to appreciate breathing.

I can't believe in a God that would be so cruel as to use disease to bring anything good to our lives. If God is Love, which many Christians are so fond of saying; wouldn't health and whole-ness be God's only agenda?

Believe in Health

As a co-creator with God, your job is to keep your attention on what you want to see more of in your life—and keep it away from what you don't want. You must be sure that your beliefs do not support or invite disease in any way.

Your beliefs may include:

1. The fear of disease. (Disease has no agenda for your life.)
2. The necessity for it as instructional in any way. (God does NOT use disease to instruct us. That's not loving!)
3. The belief that a disease has power over you. (Disease has no power over you.)

The truth is: Nothing has power over you! There is no power *over* us—only a power moving *through* us. God is that power and it is a power for GOOD only! Dr. Ernest Holmes wrote, "Never look at that which you do not wish to experience." This includes gaping at car wrecks, watching sleazy films, or listening to negative peo-ple. Be as selective as to what you let enter your mind as you are to whom you let enter your house.

Look at what you WANT! Talk about what you WANT! Think about what you WANT! Embody the idea of your desire. (i.e., If you want a friend, *be* a friend; if you want love, then *be* loving. If you want health, get involved with healthy people and healthy ideas.)

Points to Remember:

• Your *spiritual* body is always perfect!
• Disease is not a power over you. It has no agenda for your

life. It has nothing to teach you. You do not improve in anyway by suffering through it.

• God does not use disease to instruct us. God is a power for GOOD only—and that does not include disease. God is love—whose only desire for our lives is health, joy, peace and ease.

It is always appropriate to think well of yourself and to love your body. Affirm every day: *I love my body. The Intelligence that moves through it knows only how to create perfection. I am healthy and vibrant!*

CHAPTER EIGHT

Transformation

"And be not conformed to this world: be ye transformed by the renewing of your mind, that ye may prove what it is that is good, and acceptable, and the perfect will of God."

—Romans 12: 2

Life is not a mistake. It is not a series of random events with no defined purpose. The universe is alive and filled with Spirit. There is an Intelligence at the helm— unfolding a Divine purpose. That purpose is to individualize life and evolve it to a point of conscious awareness. The "will" of God is to Self-express through individualized centers of God-awareness.

As spiritual beings living in physical bodies, our destiny is clear. Inevitably, we must be transformed. At some point, the inner must be revealed on the outer. Our inherent possibility must be demonstrated in our day-to-day lives. The infinite spiritual potential that we hold inside must inevitably make its way to the outer perimeter of our lives revealing what Spirit has created us to be. In other words: Transformation is your destiny!

It is the nature of life to transform itself. Caterpillars transform themselves into butterflies. Tadpoles transform themselves into frogs. And human embryos become adults. Everything in nature is in a constant state of change. We are designed by our Creator to go as far as we can in our current shape, and then to transform into something new, leaving our former, limited self behind. This transformation is not always *physical* in nature.

Most people agree that the person they are today is not the same as the person they were five or ten years ago. Their thoughts, feelings, and priorities have changed. They see things differently and have grown out of certain behaviors. This change isn't just the result of growing older. It is an effect of spiritual maturation.

We are designed by our Creator to eclipse our former selves and become something more than we have been. We are made to let out this infinite well of being that we have inside. And as we do, we naturally achieve greater wisdom and depth. We become more loving and understanding. We develop compassion and learn to trust. When we let out what we have inside, more of God is revealed in the world and we fulfill our destiny of transformation.

Already, just a few years into the 21st century, many of our institutions, governmental structures and religious organizations are in varying states of change. Old paradigms and systems are breaking down. They no longer fulfill the purpose they were designed to serve.

All of this is a result of our own individual transformation. As individuals change, we demand similar change within our organizations. Old ways of doing things become quickly outdated and must be replaced with new models.

Our new social conscience calls on us to create only win/win paradigms. When we see that the universe and everything in it comes from the same Source, we can no longer compartmentalize our successes, or accept a course of action that allows one person to win, while someone else loses. We have to find a way where everyone can succeed.

As the old society breaks down, rigid boundaries between whites and blacks, rich and poor, Christians and non-Christians become blurred. The new diversity calls on us to accept our differences and celebrate the ONE life that runs through every person. As we do this, we learn that instead of one race or religion being right, while the other is wrong—ALL roads lead back to the same Source and ALL people are creations of Spirit, each holding equal value.

We cannot avoid this transformation! As the Borg would say on the series *Star Trek: The Next Generation*, "Resistance is futile!" It has been preprogrammed by our Creator to occur first, individually—and then collectively within us all. Spirit is awakening in the world—one life at a time—wanting to express all that it is. Day by day, it becomes clearer that the only solution is love. The only answer is unity. The only lasting peace will come from inviting everyone to the table of good.

Your desire for a better life is God-in-you waking up to what's possible for you. Your unwillingness to settle for less than what you really want is God-in-you knowing its worth. Your dissatisfaction for old, limited ways of thinking that would allow one group to have power and resources over another is God-in-you knowing we're all ONE.

You aren't finished with your work here on earth until you discover the greatness you have within you—and then show it to the world. You have a spiritual obligation to your Creator to live the very best life you can imagine. It's not too late. There's still time.

TRANSFORMING OUR LIVES

When we turn away from being a victim in life and begin to understand the Divine potential we have inside, a shift happens in our awareness. We start to see things differently. Instead of seeing life full of obstacles, we begin to feel the power of possibility rise up from within our souls. Instead of walking through life as a helpless victim waiting for the next bad thing to happen, we start thinking about what we want to happen—and how we can work toward it.

We become "action oriented" people, out there in the world, passionately pursuing our best ideas. We become co-creative partners. We develop a vision for our lives and an action plan to fulfill it. And perhaps the greatest benefit of this shift in our awareness is that we rekindle our enthusiasm for life. We return to the hopefulness we felt as a child. We feel more joy than we've felt in years.

Be forewarned that when this happens, the cynics and critics will rear their ugly heads. They will try to pierce the bubble of your newly acquired awareness. And it's important to understand *why* they do this because it will help you deal with it more effectively and with less resentment.

When they see you change and become more optimistic about life, they become fearful. When your conversations start to be more positive, they will be quick to point out all of the negatives. When you tell them your dream, they will tell you all of the reasons why your dream will never come true.

And they do this because they lost hope a long time ago— and they don't want you to have any. They bought into the idea of themselves as powerless victims, and they don't want to hear anything different from what they've already accepted, because it challenges them to rethink their belief system. And that's something they are desperately trying to avoid!

Victims are on a merry-go-round of thinking that continues to create the conditions that will repeat their experience of helplessness—and they don't want you to get off the ride they're on. They believe that by putting you down, somehow they are lifted up. In other words: If YOU can't make your dreams come true, it helps them rationalize their own failure in doing so.

So, don't look to people in the world for your happiness or

joy. Don't look to the world to support your dreams. Look to God! Go directly to the Source of your dreams for ideas on how to fulfill them. Learn to trust Spirit!

There comes a time in every person's life when you finally realize you can't depend on people to provide your good. You have to move beyond the limited resources of human beings into an infinite Source. This is a difficult process for many because it calls on us to trust in Spirit—an invisible presence we can't see or hear. But that is the purpose of all of our experiences and challenges in life—to bring us face to face with God!

TRANSFORMING OUR PERCEPTIONS

Ancient scripture warns us not to judge by appearances because things aren't always as they appear. The reflection we see in the mirror doesn't tell the full story of who we are, anymore than a glossy magazine photo of an apple is really an apple. It's just the "image" of an apple. The "image" of our body reflects in the mirror—but we can't see the full picture of ourselves, because most of what we are is invisible.

Our thoughts and feelings are not visible. Our dreams can't be seen. Our experiences of love and joy, though they may feel very real to our hearts, do not reflect in a photograph. And even though our greatest fear may play itself out in a dramatic nightmare that causes us to wake up in a sweat, the only shape or form it really takes is in our minds. We are Spirits living through physical form. Only the form is visible. Everything else lies unseen to the naked eye.

Even the experiences we call "real," such as our childhood history or memories, are often quite relative. No two children growing up with the same parents under the same social conditions will have the same experience. No two people sitting in the same movie in seats right next to each other will come away with the same perception. Our experience of life is as individualized as our own DNA. It's all a matter of perception! And since we each have a different seat in the same arena, each of us will see life from a different angle.

We never really see life for what it truly is. We see if from our own perspective. We see life the same way we see the universe from a telescope on earth. We look through the thick haze of our own atmosphere and make our judgments based on the small portion that's visible. That's why we're told not to judge by appearances, because the way we see it isn't the way it really is.

To suppose that you have the whole picture of reality is a very egotistical position. That's why it's often wise to stay away from people who claim to have the "whole" truth or the "final" revelation. Usually they are fearful people who just need to be right—and have no problem making you wrong—so they can feel more secure.

What You "See" Is What You Get

Quantum physics showed us that the results of every experiment will change based on the observer's expectations. This teaches us that there is some greater force in life that responds to our perceptions by instantly creating a reality based on our expectations. In other words, our experience of life comes from whatever belief we hold in mind. People who expect life to be good will have a good life. And people who expect life to be miserable will usually find something to be miserable about. What we expect life to be somehow shows up in our world.

This doesn't mean that we create all of reality. It does however, mean that we create our own "little" reality—our own "personal" experience of life. If you are looking at life through "rose-colored glasses," everything will look rosy. But if your perspective is jaded and clouded over by past negativity, you will see your present life the same way you view the past.

This is why we tend to create the same experiences over and over again. Because until our perspective of life changes, we can only continue to recreate the past. The names and faces may change, but the experience remains the same! Anyone who's been married more than once knows exactly what I mean. While the person you married is *different*, the relationship may be exactly the same as the last one.

The way to avoid regurgitating past experiences over and over again lies in your ability to imagine! Even Einstein himself said that imagination is more important than knowledge. Knowledge is simply a record of events that have already taken place. They are dead facts. But the power of your mind to imagine a future different from what you're living today is where your salvation lies. Unlike any other species on earth, we have the power of vision—enabling us to dramatically change the course of our lives the very instant we realize a greater wisdom.

Start "seeing" your life differently. Stop defining who you are today by what happened to you in the past. You don't have to limit your future, just because you had experiences in your past that weren't very good. You have the power to overcome your history and create a future filled with everything you didn't get in the past.

The Power of Social Conditioning

Every day we are bombarded with images of the perfect man or woman. We see them spread over billboards the size of houses. They blast their way into our living rooms via the television. And now they're digitally reproduced on millions of websites across the Internet.

Whether we're consciously aware of it or not, these images affect our lives. If left unchallenged in our minds, they become the standards by which we measure our success in life, love and career. And of course, they're completely unobtainable! No one can maintain the "perfect" waist size throughout their entire life. It's not the end of the world if your kitchen floor doesn't have the gloss of polished marble, or your hips aren't the size of a teen-age girl.

That's the sickness in our society. We keep striving to be something that doesn't exist. It's just an image reflected in cyber-space. That's why many people feel so inadequate without under-standing why. Thirty-, forty- and fifty-year-old women compare their faces and bodies to the air brushed 16-year-old they see on the cover of *Cosmopolitan* magazine. Middle-aged men work out vigorously to obtain the perfect abs they see on the guy on the cover of *Men's Health*. And when we see our own reflection in the mirror, we just don't measure up.

The truth is: You are NOT your body. Your body is nothing more than a vehicle for your spirit. It's not meant to maintain the same shape or look throughout your life. In fact, aging teaches us to assess our value in different places. And it challenges our vanity. Our bodies are supposed to grow old—and then one day, require more maintenance than we are willing to provide.

Unfortunately, our society values a person with a "good" body more than it does someone who has learned how to love. It sees only the outer perimeter of our being—and never goes below the shallow surface of our skin. It says that we are successful if we own all of the right stuff or live in the right neighborhood. But the greater truth is: Our success has to be measured by how much love, joy and freedom we have in our lives, not how much stuff we own or how much we weigh.

TRANSFORMING OUR COMMUNICATIONS

In the beginning was the *word* and the word was God. Words are powerful! Words are dangerous! Words express ideas, and ideas change lives. The words we choose express our intentions and desires. And they also expose our own belief systems. We can't hide what we truly are. It seeps out in our conversations. It reveals itself in what we say, and what we don't say.

The way we communicate with others either uplifts them or dishonors them. Our communications are either life-affirming or life-depreciating. Life is cyclical—so the words we send out come back to us! And, what we say to others, on some level, we are also saying to ourselves.

Words can empower people and call them to support great visions. Throughout our history, the world has been blessed by a few men and women who understood that power and chose to use it to uplift and empower others—people such as Martin Luther King, Jr. and Eleanor Roosevelt. But the world has also been cursed by a few who used their words for destructive purposes—Adolph Hitler and Joseph Stalin. Both are examples of the power of the word—one used for constructive means and the other for destructive.

The great American philosopher Ralph Waldo Emerson said that our language is vulgar—that it is a vain attempt to express what we truly are. He may have been right, but it's the only means we currently possess of sharing the thoughts and feelings we hold inside. And if we are to become something greater on the "outside" of life, we must first discover that greatness within—and then find some way to communicate it to the world.

How to Remain a Victim

"See, I told you I was sick!"
—Tombstone inscription in Key West

A friend of mine who comes from an experience of life that she calls "deeply scripted in the victim consciousness," was watching the evening news cast recently. And she decided to tally on a piece of paper how many times the word "victim" was used in the half-hour program. She was astonished when she added up the results. The word victim was spoken forty-two times! And that's just in one evening newscast! Imagine how many times the word is spoken on all of the programs televised in a single day.

This is why we remain victims in life—because there's a tremendous amount of support for it in our culture. And there's a lot of language that reinforces that mentality. You can be a victim of: a bad marriage, an abusive relationship, a violent crime, a poor childhood, a disease, a disaster, poverty, a mean boss, etc., etc., etc.

There is no shortage of victims in the world. Just look around. Watch Jerry Springer! It doesn't take any effort to be a victim, if that's what you want to be. So, if you want to remain one, you don't have to do a thing. The tendency of the race will automatically take over and pull you in.

However, if you want to be a co-creator instead of a victim, then you have a lot of work to do. You have to become an exception to the rule. You have to begin to "re-language" yourself in a way that supports a person who is taking his/her power back. In other words, start speaking more about what you want to be, and less about what you don't!

Stop using phrases like:

They won't let me. I can't afford it. I hope. I wish. If only I could. I'll try.

That kind of language places power outside of you and will continue to hold you in a victim consciousness. Power is INSIDE of you—where Spirit has placed it! Start using the power of your word to uplift, inspire and empower. Use your language to rebuild your life and support your faith.

Use phrases like:

When I don't know what to do, something in me does. Up until now, I haven't been able to do that, but NOW I'm ready to overcome my past. I can do anything I set my mind to do. I don't have to "hope" that my life improves, or "try" to make it so. I KNOW it will because the only power there is in the universe is a power for GOOD!

The truth is: You are now, and have always been a powerful co-creator! The invisible Energy that surrounds you is highly impressionable. Your thought impresses it like a seed planted in the soil. When your word is spoken, that Energy goes to work creating the circumstances in your life that exactly match what you've said.

That's why it's so important to watch what you say. That's why it's so important to speak only words that you really want to demonstrate in your life. Listen to what you say. Be conscious of the words you speak. And if you catch yourself saying things that continue to limit your life and keep you in a victim's experience, be gentle with yourself as you learn to "re-language" your words.

Blah, Blah, Blah

On her way back from the ladies' room, a businesswoman ran into another member of the audience. Wondering whether to reenter the lecture hall, she asked, *"Has the speaker finished what he had to say yet?"*

"Oh yeah, he finished that five minutes ago," came the reply, *"but he's still talking."*

Have you noticed how much people talk, but how little they actually say? A recent survey discovered that the topic people most discuss is the weather! Doesn't it seem peculiar that we spend so much time talking about the one thing none of us can actually do anything about?

What *should* we be talking about? How about the way we feel, or the things we think? What if we got together and had some "high level" discussions on how to heal our lives and revitalize our world? What if we talked to our children about drugs, alcohol and addiction? What if we felt comfortable enough to share our truth, our pain, or our fears? What if we told each other the stories of how we face our challenges and meet our problems? How do you think our relationships would be different if we spent our valuable time communicating things that really matter in life, instead of idle chit chat?

In his essay on friendship, Ralph Waldo Emerson wrote: "We have a great deal more kindness than is ever spoken." Even the nice things we have to say about each other often times get left unsaid.

God gave you a mouth to use. Speak up! Tell the world what you think. Stop hiding your feelings. Tell the world your vision. Start talking about what you really want. Express yourself! Use the power of your word to talk about things that really matter—things you want to see more of in your life and in the world. And if you want to know about the weather, watch the weather channel.

Honest To God

When I was a kid and I wanted adults to really believe what I was telling them, I would end every sentence by saying, "honest to God!" We inherently know that God would never lie to us or lead us down the wrong path—honest to God!

So, what if we followed our Creator's example? What if we only had *honest* communications? Do you think it's possible to speak the truth all of the time? Do you think it's even socially acceptable?

I have a friend who gets "stuck" a lot. And when she does, she comes to me first, because she knows I'll tell her the truth. Some of her other friends tell her what they think she wants to hear. Some will give her their opinion. And others will remain silent, because they don't want to hurt her feelings. But I'm completely honest with her and always tell her the truth—with large doses of compassion and love. That's the key: compassion and love! You don't have to be cruel, unkind or judgmental to be honest.

I think we owe our friends honesty. Because they're based in love, all friendships should also be based in truth. So I tell my friends the truth when they ask, and I expect the same from them as well. If a friend sees me going down the wrong path, I want them to speak up and tell me. Don't let me go places I don't need to go and waste valuable time and resources. Tell me the truth—I can take it!

It really is possible to be honest in all of our communications. In fact, it can be very empowering to do so. Here are a few examples:

Try this at Home

The next time someone calls that you don't really want to speak to, instead of having a family member lie to the other person telling them you're not home, have them say something like:

She/He is here but has had a challenging day so he/she is taking some time alone right now. Can I have her/him call you back later?

Try this at Work

The next time an employer asks you what you think of the new company policy, instead of telling him/her what you think he/she wants to hear, say something like:

I believe you employ me here because what I have to contribute makes the company better, so instead of telling you what I think you "want" to hear, let me tell you what I honestly think. And please know that I'm not wedded to this opinion. It can change.

Try this with a Friend

The next time a friend asks for your opinion about some action they're ready to take, and you believe it wouldn't be the best choice for them, say something like:

I love you—and I only want the best for you. So, I'm going to tell you the truth. I don't think that would be a good choice for you. Of course, you have to make your own decisions because it's your life. And whatever you choose, I'm still going to love you and want the best for you.

Try this with a Relative

The next time a relative calls trying to make you feel guilty for something you've done or not done, say something like:

You know, guilt used to work well on me. I used to listen to you and then hang up the phone feeling pretty bad about myself— and then make sure I took a long time before I ever called you back. But that doesn't work for me any more and I'd like to begin building a new relationship with you based on truth and love—not guilt and manipulation...

✳ THE FUTURE OF OUR COMMUNICATIONS

One of the most popular books in recent time is *Men are from Mars, Women are from Venus*. In it the author, John Gray, speaks about the communication barrier between genders. Of course, it helps us to understand that men and women communicate differently. But it's also heavily generalized. Communication differences don't necessarily occur because of our gender. They happen because we're all unique individuals who think, act, and feel differently from each other. Everyone expresses love differently. Everyone has a different experience of loss and grief. No one feels or expresses their feelings exactly the way you do.

Modern science has created devices that record our voices. We can play a tape recording of someone singing or talking. And we can see images of that same person on a videotape or DVD. We can even read what they've written on the printed page. But we can't get inside their head or their heart. We can't really know what's on their mind!

Perhaps one day we'll create a device that records our thoughts and feelings exactly as they occur inside our own mind/heart. And then the world will truly be transformed—because then we could share our recording with others. We could use them to help resolve major issues in the world. The Arabs could finally see how the Jews feel. The Protestants would truly understand the Catholic perspective. And the people you love will finally understand exactly how you feel!

Can you imagine a world where people really knew how you felt? Can you imagine the closeness we would feel toward another person, and the oneness of all humanity? Can you imagine the compassion we would all have for each other?

You can begin to experience that transformation in your relationships by committing yourself to honesty right now. Tell the truth more often. Even if it stings a little bit at first, in the long run you'll find that people will really respect you for it.

TRANSFORMING OUR WORLD

"Remember, we are all affecting the world every moment, whether we mean to or not. Our actions and states of mind matter, because we're so deeply interconnected with one another. Working on our own consciousness is the most important thing that we are doing at any moment, and being love is the supreme creative act."

—Ram Dass

The first call to transformation is personal and individual. Each person has to begin the process with an awakening to their own identity as a spiritual being. No one can do this for us. It is a process that must evolve in its own time and sequence. It can't be scheduled or enforced. The awakening process may take months or years to unfold as we make new discoveries and learn to assimilate spiritual principles into our daily lives.

Healing old wounds, overcoming past resentments and realigning ourselves with more authentic living must be our first priority. And it is an ongoing effort that requires daily attention to stay centered in peace and wholeness—particularly in the confused and chaotic world we live in. Our first responsibility then must be to ourselves—to maintain a *consciousness* that is loving and peaceful.

But once we have our support system intact, and daily practices established to help maintain our spiritual awareness, then we hear the second call to transformation.

This call is global and is a call of service for all humankind. With our new-found identity comes an awareness of the interconnectedness of all life and an understanding that what we do to others, we also do to ourselves. This new awareness causes us to begin working for a better world, not just a better life for ourselves.

Creating a World in which You Want to Live

"We are a future-creating species, the great futurist Fred Polak wrote in 1955. Our future is not merely something that happens to us but something that we participate in creating. If we do this consciously, we can create a world that works."

—Dr. Paul Ray, Sherry Anderson, *The Cultural Creatives*

Without a positive vision for our future, we cannot succeed. The Dark Ages and the Renaissance were merely two options available to a culture—one showing the negative and the other the positive. We can have despair and closed-mindedness or we can have open creativity. The choice is ours.

Now is the time to develop a great vision for our world. We need visionaries now more than ever! We need people to imagine cities that are safe and community-friendly. We need new businesses that are environmentally friendly that don't exploit third-world people. We need politicians who understand spiritual principles and practice them in their daily lives. We need people to envision a sustainable economy that invites everyone to the table of prosperity.

The world can be anything we want it to be. We have the power to create it from the vision we hold inside—if we have faith in our vision and keep looking for ways to bring it into fruition.

According to philosopher David Spangler, a positive vision of the future "challenges the culture to dare, to be open to change, and to accept a spirit of creativity that could alter its very structure." We are on the verge of that kind of dramatic change in our world today.

The very structure of our society is being altered in ways that past generations couldn't even imagine. It may take a few decades to come about, but the work we do is worthwhile because it creates a better life for future generations. It honors the chain of creation that extends beyond our own human life span.

Can you imagine a world where wealth is more evenly distributed among nations? Can you imagine a world where all of our assets are used toward the betterment of our people, instead of building up military arsenals? Can you imagine a world where education and information are free for all citizens? Can you imagine a government system that honors every religion, race or creed as holding equal value and rights? Can you imagine an economy that is sustainable and an environment that is vigorously protected?

Those who can envision a positive image for our future are the ones responsible for enacting it. You hold the key to the world's future in YOUR mind! How will you use that key?

PLACE THE OXYGEN MASK ON YOURSELF FIRST

After the September 11th national tragedy, suddenly everyone started listening to the announcements that flight attendants give just prior to take off. Before then, everyone just tried to ignore them.

One of the fundamental rules is: "Should the cabin lose pressure, oxygen masks will automatically fall from overhead. If you are traveling with small children, place the oxygen mask on yourself first and then on your child." Someone who's supposed to know these things told me the reason why that's so important. Apparently, as the cabin loses pressure, you only have a few seconds before everyone passes out. So, if you try to place the oxygen mask on your child first, you will probably pass out and not be able to help them any further, much less help yourself.

There's a great lesson in this. You can't be of help to anyone else until YOU help yourself first. You can't heal others until YOUR life is healed. You can't guide others to balanced, functional relationships until YOU know how to demonstrate them in your own life. Only the rich can help the poor and only the well can help the sick. YOU have to create a balanced life first, before you can be a positive influence on others.

In the Sixties I had an idealistic friend who set out to heal the world. A couple of decades later, I ran into him in Atlanta, Georgia. He was just the opposite of his former self. His idealism had turned to cynicism and his joyful anticipation turned into expecting the absolute worst from life. He had no money, no fulfilling relationship of any kind and no particular career. His life was completely out of balance! Unfortunately, he made the mistake that a lot of people make. He set out to heal the world without first healing himself.

To fulfill your soul's assignment here on earth, your first order of business is to get YOUR life in order. Heal your resentments. Forgive yourself for past mistakes. Heal your body image. Get your financial life in order. Raise your self esteem. Create a balanced life for yourself first—and then you will be a positive influence on others and a good candidate for love.

CHAPTER NINE

The Balanced Life

❋ Row, Row, Row Your Boat

Living in natural harmony with Spirit is like floating down a gentle stream allowing the current to carry you to whatever destination the water dictates. It is a place of complete trust and total surrender! Instead of making life happen, you permit and allow it to unfold. Instead of forcing your good from a reluctant and stingy world, you become an "instrument" of good in the world. Instead of "worshipping" a distant God—you become ONE with Spirit!

Do you remember the childhood, sing-a-long song "Row Your Boat?" There's a powerful lesson about balance and harmony in that little song. In case you've forgotten, here is the verse. Sing it, instead of reading it:

> "Row, row, row your boat
> Gently down the stream
> Merrily, merrily, merrily, merrily,
> life is but a dream!"

The first line of the song reminds us where to place our attention and effort in life. It says: "Row, row, row YOUR boat." That means we should give all of our attention to our own issues and challenges—and not waste time sticking our noses into other people's business.

Focus your attention on resolving YOUR issues. Don't get into some else's boat and try to do their "rowing." You have enough work of your own to get through. You don't need the distraction. Plus, it will divert your attention away from your own course. Row, row, row YOUR boat.

The second line of the song, "gently down the stream," reminds us that life isn't supposed be a struggle. We're not supposed to fight our way "upstream" with the salmon. The flow of life is "downstream." If you're applying an inordinate amount of effort to make or force something to happen in your life, then you're going about it the wrong way. Stop! Back off—and allow the natural flow of life to take over. Remember that life wants to work. Good wants to be expressed. You aren't responsible for making it happen. Row your boat "gently" down the stream!

The third line of the song reminds us that life is designed for joy! We're supposed to be having a good time, not working ourselves to death. That's why there are only three "rows..." in the song. And yet, there are four "merrilys..." That's to teach us that our efforts at rowing should not exceed the joy we receive from our work. In other words, if it's not fun, it's not really worth doing! Do what you love. Give your efforts to something you can pour your heart in to. Life isn't about how much you can accomplish or how many tasks you can cross off your to-do-list. It's supposed to be a joyful adventure!

And finally, the last line— life is but a dream —reminds us not to take it all too personally, or too seriously. The dramas and traumas of our lives are all self-created stories designed to draw out our inner potential. They're just chapters in the eternal unfolding of our souls. The conditions of our lives do NOT define who we are. They're just signposts along the way. You are NOT your work. You are NOT your house. You are NOT your money. You are a perfect expression of God on a spiritual journey of discovery. This "human life" is just one experience along the way. Don't take it too seriously. It's just a dream!

⊱ BALANCED LIFE

"What lies behind us and what lies before us are tiny matters compared to what lies within us."

— Oliver Wendell Holmes

What we have within us is the perfect, balanced and whole life of Spirit. It animates our bodies, sustains our lives, and restores our soul. It is a point of "perfect center" from which our lives are created. When we are in alignment with that "center," we live a balanced and healthy life. However, when we venture too far to the right or left, we become imbalanced. Inevitably, the choice is ours. We are responsible for setting our own course in life and making our own choices.

Creating a balanced life means making *conscious* choices. It requires clear intentions and discipline. Instead of letting your schedule control you, why not control your schedule? Instead of being a victim to all of your appointments and activities, why not arrange them giving equal time and validity to appointments of self-care?

Caring for yourself is a sign of healthy self-esteem. Extreme self-care is a sign of great self-love. The bottom line is: We take care of what we *value* the most. We give special attention to the people and things we love. So, the question is: What are you doing to care for yourself? How do you show self-love? Do you schedule regular massages or facials? Do you have appointed times to listen to music or walk in nature? Do you exercise and eat well? Or, do you use the same old excuse that there's not enough time?

As physical beings, we need food to stay alive. It nourishes our bodies and sustains our lives. But as spiritual beings, we need love and laughter. It "feeds" our spirit and sustains our wholeness. Without love and laughter, we become spiritually dis-eased which, if left unchecked will eventually result in some physical dis-ease.

Living a balanced life means making choices that honor your spirit's need for love and joy. It means taking time away from your regular schedule to do the things you love, and to be with people who make you laugh. It means valuing yourself enough to put your own needs first and foremost in life.

I have a friend who is a classic co-dependent and when I advise her to take special care of herself, she says, "It sounds so selfish! I always feel guilty when I take time for myself." Her programming has always been to care for others *before* she cares for herself. And she continues to do this to her own detriment. Her life is out of order. She is worn out and desperate—but everyone around her is happy and fulfilled—because she's given everything she had away.

Unless you create a specific plan of self-care, it will be too easy to fall back into self-destructive habits. Old habits can be broken. You can rise above your programming—but you will need a plan.

GET A PLAN

Create a daily, weekly and monthly care plan. Write down at least three things you are willing to do to take care of yourself and your family. For example: Your Daily Care Plan might include prayer and meditation. It may include an hour with the kids just messing around with the television turned off.

Your Weekly Care Plan might include a date night with your partner or a family night with the kids. It might include a trip to the park or some other outing in nature. Your Monthly Care Plan might include a massage, a movie, dinner in a new restaurant, or a family day-trip in the car. In the space provided, create your own plan:

Daily Care Plan

1._____

2._____

3._____

Weekly Care Plan

1._____

2._____

3._____

Monthly Care Plan

1._____

2._____

3._____

❊ MORE, MORE, MORE

We are consumed by our consumer-based culture! We were socially conditioned as children to want the newest, latest and shiniest toys. And that conditioning followed us all the way into adulthood. We continue to search for happiness outside ourselves through the pursuit of more money, better jobs, newer things and more expensive toys. And once we're on the merry-go-round of MORE, MORE, MORE, it's hard to get off. So, we have to keep working harder and harder just to keep up.

The dangling carrot of true happiness always remains in front of us, somewhere up ahead, in a place we never quite get to. And we keep chasing after it like an addict after a drug. We take second and third jobs. We start new companies and work part-time at home. Work invades every area of our lives until we no longer know where *it* ends and *we* begin. And if we stop working, we don't know what else to do. We've defined our value and purpose by it for so long, that without it, we no longer have an identity. So, we keep working to keep feeling valuable.

The truth is: The value of our lives doesn't increase or decrease based on the fluctuation of our assets. We will never gain self-worth through ownership. Self worth comes from an inner knowing of who you are and your spiritual connection to the universe. It has nothing to do with your station in life or how much buying power you have. It has nothing to do with your resume or job title.

God doesn't care where you work, what you drive or how you dress! Spirit designed you to live well, be happy, express yourself and explore love. Life is supposed to be an adventure story—not a race to see who gets more stuff first.

DO LESS, BE MORE

What difference does it make how much you get done, if what you're doing isn't what matters the most to you? Who cares what you accomplish, if everyone gets abused in the process, including you? Don't busy your life with unsatisfying social engagements, obligatory commitments and mundane tasks. Stop victimizing yourself with a frenzied schedule.

Take time daily to reflect on what's really important to you. Feed your spirit by listening to music that moves your heart. Take walks. Exercise your body. Meditate in silence. Consider the "big picture." Think about what you care about the most and what makes your life meaningful. Envision a greater future. Dream! Create!

Living in harmony is about recognizing yourself first as a spiritual being—not a human *doer.*

Some Simple Questions to Ask Yourself

- What is complicating my life right now?
- Is it my job, boss, coworkers, or outside obligations?
- Am I spending too much time working, commuting, or volunteering to do things that I don't really want to do?
- What would bring greater peace to my life?
- What could I stop doing or give up that would create more free time?

THE "JUST BE" MEDITATION

"Why should the lord of the country flit like a fool? If you let yourself be blown to and fro, you lose touch with your root. If you let restlessness move you, you've lost touch with who you are."

—Lao Tzu

The ancient Eastern wisdom of the Tao says, "Do less, BE more." Our soul longs to return to the simple pleasures of our childhood when *joy* was our main priority and *loving* was our only career—a time when we had less to *do* and more to *be*.

You will never have a peaceful life if you keep running around in circles. You have to slow down and stop the panic long enough for serenity to catch up with you. Peace and serenity can't be found in chaos. They are found deep *within* your soul. They are natural effects of living a *balanced* life.

Set aside time each day to just "BE." Start off with five minutes the first week. And then move up in five-minute increments each week until you reach thirty minutes of just "being" time. Sit perfectly still and allow yourself to be FULLY PRESENT right where your body is. When your attention wanders, bring it gently back to the present moment. Watch the moments unfold and pass.

Like anything else that is new, in the beginning it may seem awkward. You may think you're not doing it "right." Your mind will wander back to "doing" instead of being. You may find yourself thinking about what there is to do next—wash the car, fold the clothes, go to the store, make dinner, etc. Be patient when this happens. Give yourself time to learn how to "BE." Lovingly bring your attention back to "Being." If you repeat this exercise daily, you will find yourself healthier, less stressful and happier!

CALGON...TAKE ME AWAY!

In order to live consciously, we have to first slow down! Enjoying simple pleasures in life takes time. Here are some suggestions:

- Instead of a quick shower, take a long, hot bubble bath.
- Turn off the television and talk to your loved ones.
- Spend an hour each day reading inspirational material.

- Play your favorite music.
- Don't watch the news before you go to bed at night.
- Consider a question that you are trying to answer and "sit" in the question. Don't rush to find an answer. Just "be" in the question.
- Let yourself feel boredom. Create space in your life where you have NOTHING to do.

VOLUNTARY SIMPLICITY

"Simplicity, simplicity, simplicity! I say let your affairs be two or three, and not a hundred or a thousand; instead of a million count half a dozen... In the midst of this chopping sea of civilian life, such are the clouds and storms and quicksands and the thousand-and-one items to be allowed for... Simplify, Simplify!"
—Henry David Thoreau, *Walden*

Give yourself the gift of a simple life. Live in the moment. Don't feel as though you have to schedule every hour or busy yourself with tasks. When you catch yourself falling into your old habit of over-doing—STOP everything! Slow down! DO ONE THING AT A TIME!

Voluntary simplicity involves doing only one thing at a time so that you are fully present in the moment. Instead of reading *and* listening to music—just read—or just listen. Instead of fumbling through the mail *and* talking on the phone—be fully present in your conversation and do nothing else. Do one thing at a time and fully engage yourself in that activity. Voluntary simplicity means to intentionally "slow everything down."

Remember that your value is not determined by how much you accomplish. You are a spiritual being. Your value comes from the presence of Spirit in you.

Trust that God has everything under control. You aren't

responsible for building an empire or "fixing" the world. Everything will get done that actually needs to get done. You can trust God to care for its creation.

Relax and enjoy life. It was given to you as a gift from the universe's greatest Lover! It is a gift that is supposed to be opened slowly and with intent. Peel it away, layer by layer—enjoying each one before you go to the next.

Celebrate your successes BEFORE you move on to the next task. Simplify your life by removing unnecessary "busy work" from your schedule. Schedule time to do nothing! Create time for love-making and joy-making.

LEARN TO VALUE THE PROCESS

There is an old Sufi story that tells the tale of modern man. In it, Nasruddin goes to a teacher for music lessons. *"How much do the lessons cost?"* he asks. *"Fifteen dollars for the first lesson, ten dollars for each one after that,"* says the teacher. And Nasruddin replies, *"I'll begin with lesson number two."*

This story gives us insight into our social programming. It shows us our usual approach to performing tasks. We want it fast and cheap! We want to get to the end of the task as quickly as possible. It's as if we're running a race and the person who arrives at death's door first, wins. And how stupid is that?

The real value in life doesn't come from accomplishing tasks or achieving goals. It comes from what you learn and how you treat people in the process. It's not what gets done that's important. It's *how* it gets done that really matters. Were the members of the group honored and respected? When the goal was achieved, did you stop long enough to acknowledge your success and celebrate it with each other? Did everyone feel empowered? Were extraordinary efforts rewarded? These are the things that are really important!

Learn to value the process more than the task. Don't focus on what gets done more than you focus on how people are treated. If you value people first and encourage them to do their best, they will be loyal and work together as a team. Use this important spiritual principle at home, work, or any other place where people come together around a common theme. It will work miracles!

You Are in Complete Control of Your Life...Sort of

If you divide a piece of paper in half and list on one side all of the things you CAN control, you'll find the list has only two things on it—your thoughts and feelings. You choose how to think and feel. You are in complete control of that, and nothing else!

This is good news because how you choose to think creates your belief system, which causes your actions, which determines what experience returns to you. Therefore, the only thing you have complete control of is the *quality* of your own life experience. Everything else in life requires your faith and trust.

Control freaks live in fear! They're afraid life will spin out of control and become unmanageable. They don't trust that there is a perfect Intelligence at the helm of this great universe—unfolding an orderly life. They think *they* are responsible for making life work. And clearly that kind of thinking is just a bit ego-centric.

Know What You Can Control and What You Can't

You are dancing with the Divine! Sometimes you get to lead, but sometimes you must follow. The trick is to know when to do what. As a co-creative, spiritual partner in life, it is your responsibility to keep your sight on the greatest good you can imagine. Do not let anything interfere with your view. Do not let any negative event "pull you away" from your intended result. No matter what happens, or "appears" to happen, keep looking at what you want.

It is God's responsibility to take what you have so faithfully believed in, and create the ways and means for it to come into fruition. God knows how to do this very well! Do not interfere by trying to figure out how your good will come to you. Do not try to control events that you know nothing about. Instead, spend your time controlling your thought. Keep it focused on the positive.

Use this affirmation to keep focused on the positive:

I am in total control of my thoughts and feelings.

God is in control of everything else—and all is well!

⚹ PRACTICE LETTING GO

- The next time you find yourself weaving through traffic frustrated and angry, instead of speeding up and pushing your way to the front of the line, get behind someone going slowly. Practice the feeling of NOT having to lead or be the one in front.

- When you catch yourself feeling frustrated because you can't control the outcome of some event—STOP, take a breath. Remember it is NOT your job to MAKE anything happen.

- Remember that good WANTS to happen. You don't have to force it or try to manipulate it. Spirit WANTS to express itself. Love WANTS to happen! Abundance WANTS to be revealed! Healing WANTS to occur! Life WANTS to work! It's a natural event that WILL take place, if nothing blocks it.

- Place the following message on a post-it somewhere visible to you each morning:

"Good Morning (Your name here), this is your Higher Power. I won't be needing YOUR help today."

⅀ FINDING PEACE AND SERENITY IN A CHAOTIC WORLD

Statistics show that the average North American works 20% *more* today than in 1973 and has 32% *less* free time per week. We are a society obsessed with activity. Every moment is filled with something to do. Between our careers, family obligations, friendships and social commitments, there's no time left to just "BE!"

We just keep running around like a chicken with its head cut off. We get up in the morning and hurry off to work—and then rush home to eat at night. Fast food has become the staple of everyone's diet. We "plate-spin" our relationships, career and family obligations—trying to keep them all up in the air without crashing down.

Our new technology was supposed to make our lives easier and give us more leisure time. But because of our increased mobility and the ever-present laptop computer and mobile phone, it has done just the opposite. Work has invaded our homes, cars, and *lunches!* The other day I was having lunch with friends in a popular restaurant and we could hardly hear each other talk over the constant ringing of mobile phones. Would it be so terrible to not be available by phone for just an hour?

All of this activity isn't making our lives any better. In fact, it's destroying them. Our frenzied lifestyle is making our children overweight and putting millions of adults on anti-depressants just to cope with the stress. We have to find some way to restore order. Bringing balance to our lives has to become a priority.

Finding time to address our physical, emotional, psychological and spiritual needs takes discipline and commitment. It calls on us to reaffirm our values and vision. In other words, we have to stop asking ourselves, *"What do we do for a living?"* and start asking, *"What are we living for?"*

⚜ You Are Not Your Job

"They intoxicate themselves with work so they won't see how they really are."

— Aldous Huxley

In her book *Take Time for Your Life*, Cheryl Richardson writes: *"Years of conditioning have taught us to look toward work for the meaning and fulfillment we desire. This is evidenced by those who call asking me for help in finding or building a career that will fulfill their 'life purpose.' Or the business owners who are anxious to get the right 'mission statement' completed so they can be on their way to living the life they're 'meant to live.'*

Expecting your work to provide you with this kind of profound meaning and fulfillment is a setup. You end up investing too much of your time and energy in work, desperately searching for something that cannot be found there—a life."

A recent study showed that out of more than four thousand male executives surveyed, 48% saw their lives as empty and meaningless despite years of hard work. This sense of emptiness brews as an underlying sadness that rises to the surface only when they take time away from work. Like a drug addict trying to avoid "coming down" off of the drug, they return to work to avoid feelings of sorrow and loss. They literally haven't got time for the pain!

Slowing down can mean unleashing pent-up emotions that have built up over time. It can be a frightful experience to stop and take a truthful look at what you're missing in life. For many misguided people, their *self* worth is directly tied to their *net* worth. So they keep chasing after success thinking "one day" they'll have enough. But of course, that day never comes—so they just "keep on truckin'," completely unaware of the trap into which they've fallen.

While it is a fact that we live in a society that values what we *do* over who we *are*, the greater truth is: You are NOT your work. Your value doesn't come from anything you accomplish or how many tasks you cross off your to-do list. You are not more attractive because you have a fancy title or a four-page resume. ALL of your value comes from the Spirit inside you!

You are valuable to God when you learn how to give and receive love—not when you receive an "Employee of the Year" award. Work is a *part* of your life. And it may be an important part. But, it is not supposed to be the most important part.

The Very Busy Woman

I know a woman who works nearly eighty hours a week. Every time you see her, she's in a rush. She never has more than a minute to say hello before she has to scurry off to her next appointment. She's one of those people who can turn a simple task into a major event, making it much more complicated than is necessary.

After observing her for awhile, her "game" was revealed to me. I learned that she had never felt important or valued as a child. And so, as a result, she grew up with very little self-esteem. She carried this wound with her into adulthood.

By taking simple tasks and making them far more complex than they ever needed to be, she could feel important and valuable for working through them. She created chaos around her so she could resolve the chaos, and then feel good about herself for resolving it. Every day of her life, she starred in a complex drama that was totally self-created as a reaction from not having enough love or attention in her childhood. Her whole script was being written completely *unconscious* of what she was doing. She was totally unaware of why her life was so chaotic.

⚜ SLOW DOWN, YOU MOVE TOO FAST

In her book, *The Circle of Simplicity*, Cecile Andrews gives us some alarming statistics: "Couples spend an average of 12 minutes a day talking to each other and 40 minutes per week playing with children." And, "half of all Americans don't get enough sleep."

With these statistics it's no wonder that many marriages end in divorce. Successful relationships are built upon constant communication. Unless you take time to talk to each other, one day you're going to wake up, look at the person next to you and wonder who they are. You can't maintain a successful relationship on 12 minutes a day!

No wonder kids join gangs. They probably do so, just to get attention from another human being. If the person you looked to for love and support only spent 40 minutes a week with you, wouldn't you look elsewhere? And we wonder why our children are so unruly and disrespectful? They're probably just starved for attention. They'll never admit it, but the truth is: Your kids need to know you love them much more than they need another video game!

The amount of time we have in a day is limited, so we have to make sure we're using it in ways that honor who we are as spiritual beings, and our significant relationships with family and friends. If we wait to care for ourselves, or the people we love when we find the time, we'll never do it. You don't find time. You TAKE time!

Slow down! You're trying to do too much—and the things that are the most important are probably being ignored.

⚜ I Just Want to Be Happy!

Those are the six words every therapist, minister and counselor hears every day in session. Their patients just want to be happy, like everybody else. And yet they don't realize that happiness is an *effect* of living a balanced life. We become happy when we have balanced our lives with:

- Relationships that are healthy outlets for giving and receiving love.
- Work that is a place of validation and compensation for our creative ideas.
- Healthy food choices to balance our body's nutrition.
- Joyful recreational activity.
- Spiritual community that connects us with others who are working to make the world a better place to live.
- Time for self-love and care.

Money doesn't make us happy. People don't make us happy. Moving to another city can't make us happy. No one and no thing can MAKE you happy, because joy isn't an *external* event. It's a natural state of mind that comes from *within*. It rises up as an effect of living in harmony with life. It comes from living a balanced life.

⚟ SETTING BOUNDARIES

In the last thirteen years, a lot of couples have come to me for counseling. And in my professional opinion, the two main reasons most relationships fail is because couples don't take enough time to be together and they don't set any boundaries.

When couples come to me for premarital counseling, I strongly suggest the following boundaries:

- No television in the bedroom, ever!
- No conversations in the bedroom about children, money or business, ever!

- Give each other "mental space" when you get home from work. We all need "decompression" time.
- Set aside at least one night a week for a "date night" allowing nothing to intervene (except emergencies).
- Create a Daily, Weekly and Monthly Care Plan for yourself and your relationship.
- Create annual goals that you both share in common.

Modern life can be stressful and overwhelming. It's too easy to let all of the activities of the day invade every conversation and location in the house. Setting a boundary of no discussions about children, money issues or business in the bedroom will save your relationship and keep the passion alive for years to come.

Refusing to put a television in the bedroom will keep you from falling into the bad habit of relying on the "the tube" for enjoyment, when you should be looking to each other. Without any troubling issues to discuss and nothing to watch on T.V., it's amazing how quickly conversations turn to what's really important and passion is automatically rekindled.

Creating space and time to be together becomes an investment in your relationship that quickly pays off. Regularly scheduled "date nights" allow time to give your full attention to each other and strengthen the bond you have together.

Boundaries are very important for keeping balance. What other boundaries can you think of that might be helpful in bringing greater success to your relationships?

❧ BALANCE YOUR RELATIONSHIPS

As peculiar as this might sound, I was recently inspired by the selection of lettuce at the supermarket: Boston lettuce, red-leaf, green-leaf, romaine, butter, field greens, and the plain, but ever-popular, iceberg. And it made me think of the variety of people in my life: white accountants, black doctors, gay therapists, male actors, female lawyers, young people, old people, rich ones and poor ones.

We've been told that the key to a healthy diet is to include a *variety* of food groups. Perhaps the key to a healthy and balanced life comes from including that same dose of variety in our relationships. If this is true, then one would seek to have friends from a variety of different cultural and ethnic groups, as well as religious and political affiliations. For balance, we would seek out relationships with people of varying age groups, race, sexual orientation and social status.

It's clear that Spirit had an *assortment* in mind when it made the human race. No single person can satisfy all of our relationship needs. That's why we have so many choices. And yet, the one thing we all share in common—and perhaps the only thing—is that we're all individual expressions of the same Spirit. Each one of us has been uniquely designed to share a special gift with the world. No one can be duplicated or replaced. Every person offers something unrepeated in nature.

Imbalance occurs when we don't have enough diversity in our lives. We were not designed to live "by bread alone." That's why relationships with our biological family should hold equal value with our chosen, spiritual family if the two aren't the same. Friendships are just as important to our psychological well-being as our families. Relationships with our pets also bring something unique to our lives that humans cannot. Variety is the key in creating a whole-life experience.

When you rely on one person or one relationship to fulfill all of your needs, you apply undo pressure on that person and create a scenario that will ultimately lead to failure. To make one person your advisor, confidant, best friend, spiritual guru and lover is not healthy. Spread yourself around. Seek out new relationships regularly. Don't depend on the same people for the same benefits.

People are fascinating creatures and each one has something new to offer you. Don't be afraid to extend yourself to them. After all, you have one very important thing in common with them—you come from the same Life!

✹ YOU ARE AN AGELESS, TIMELESS BEING

"The final mystery is oneself. When one has weighed the sun in the balance, and measured the steps of the moon, and mapped out the seven heavens star by star, there still remains oneself. Who can calculate the orbit of his own soul?"

—Oscar Wilde, *De Profundis*

You are not your body! You are the occupant of it. You are the ageless, timeless being living through it. As a spiritual being you have *spiritual* needs. Living in harmony with life requires you to address them. As a spiritual being you have a need to connect to a purpose greater than your own ego-agenda. Inherently you know it's your obligation to leave the world in better shape than you found it.

Once you've reconnected with your soul's assignment to love, the next step in living a balanced life is to align that purpose with others. Join a spiritual community that is making a difference in the world. Find causes that you believe in and support them. Connect with other people on a regular basis who recognize themselves as spiritual beings. These spiritual relationships are important in realizing a balanced life. Don't underestimate their value.

Peace of mind comes from knowing your purpose in life and then fulfilling it. It comes from knowing you're making a difference in the world—that because you are alive, somehow things improve. The quality of life on the planet is raised each time you honor that purpose. The value of who you are doesn't come from what you accomplish or how much you acquire. It comes from being what Spirit created you to be and sharing that uniqueness with the world in a positive, uplifting way.

WHAT IT FEELS LIKE TO LIVE IN HARMONY WITH LIFE

I went whitewater rafting in Tennessee with a group of friends several years ago. All six of us were very close, having spent many years together. With our trained guide on the raft, we courageously set out on an adventure that was new for each of us. As the rapids tossed us from side to side, we quickly learned how to paddle together, three of us on one side of the raft paddling one direction and three of us on the other side paddling another. This allowed us to move through the rapids harmoniously without overturning the raft.

We had a blast! It was one of those days where everything was just perfect. The weather was beautiful. The sun was shining and the water was so clear that you could see the bottom of the river. And what made it most fun was being with the people I loved the most, sharing a new adventure with friends for whom I really cared.

After a few hours of battling the rapids, we finally came to a place of perfect calm in the river—a place where the current flowed slowly and gently. At this point, our guide told us it was safe to get out of the raft and swim.

After swimming separately for a few minutes we found ourselves face to face in the water, slowing moving downstream talking about the day's exciting adventure. That's when we decided to create a special ritual to solidify our bond of friendship and commemorate that special day. On our backs in the water, we formed a circle, held hands as we floated down the river and sang, "What the world needs now is love, sweet love..."

I'll never forget the experience: In a safe place, feeling my body submerged in water, floating gently down stream, holding hands with the people who meant the most to me in life, staring up at the clear, blue sky, singing together. It was one of the best days of my life!

Later it occurred to me that what I felt that day must be exactly what it feels like to live in harmony with life (Spirit). To feel completely safe and cared for, without having to apply any hard effort, allowing the current to carry you to wonderful places you can't schedule on your own. Being surrounded by love and beauty, and so moved by the grandeur of it all that you spontaneously start to sing for joy.

Like a river, there is a "current" in life, a natural flowing of Spirit. When we fight it and try to make it on our own, it's like swimming up stream. Eventually the effort we have to apply wears us down. Exhausted and desperate, we finally surrender and let the "spiritual current" carry us.

Like everything else in life, we have a choice. We can try to fight our way upstream—or we can let go, and let Spirit gently carry us to our destiny. God is a power for *good* in the universe and the eternal presence of unconditional Love! Its only desire is for your highest good.

Your soul's assignment is to express *all* that God is—love, joy, ease, peace and prosperity. That's the life God designed for you to live. But since the first gift of love is *freedom,* you are free to choose for yourself whether or not to honor your Creator's intention.

Harmony resides with those who choose to align themselves with the flow of the universe. People who live harmonious lives are in synchronicity with Spirit. Its course becomes *their* course. Instead of blindly pursuing their own ego-agenda, they remain flexible and open to new possibilities. They worry less. They rarely panic. They live in faith, and trust that no matter what shows up in life, they are in the presence of a power whose only intention for their lives is to unfold the highest good. They are not afraid to "float" on their own.

YOU ARE A MENTAL, EMOTIONAL, PHYSICAL, SPIRITUAL BEING

We are multifaceted beings with multiple needs. As *mental* beings, we have a need for intellectual stimulation and wisdom. As *emotional* beings, we have a need for emotional support from those around us. As *physical* beings, we need air, food, water and shelter to survive. And as *spiritual* beings, we need to feel connected to Spirit. Balance comes from allowing time for each category of needs.

We've all seen people who have overdeveloped bodies and underdeveloped minds. The world is full of highly skilled people who lack basic spiritual wisdom. We have many examples around us in our daily lives of people living imbalanced lives. It is a common experience. That's why there are so many unhappy people *trying* to act happy and so many angry people *trying* to be nice.

By giving our time, attention and resources to each area, we create balance and harmony in our lives. Inner stability comes from addressing yourself as a *whole* person with multiple needs. Fulfilling your soul's assignment requires you to live consciously, making choices that honor yourself as a *spiritual being.*

CHAPTER TEN

What's Really Important: Your Soul's Assignment

HONOR YOUR RELATIONSHIP WITH SPIRIT

The first and most important relationship in your life is with your Creator! When your relationship with Spirit is not cultivated and secured, it is nearly impossible to have a healthy relationship with anyone else.

The most significant question we each have to answer for ourselves is: What *kind* of God do I believe in? And here's a clue: The answer to this question is NOT in a book or a Bible. It can't be answered by another person or an institution. The answer lies in your own *heart* awaiting your discovery.

My answer may not be yours. But I offer it for your review and consideration:

The only things we truly value in life are the times and the people we love. Love is the only thing we feel compelled to communicate when we're at the end of life. We want people to know that we loved them—and we need to know that we've been loved in return.

Love is empowering! When we feel loved, we feel empowered. It makes us feel as though we could conquer the world. Love brings us joy. When we're in love, we're happy and our hearts are full.

God is LOVE! God is not a loving *Being*. God is Love, ITSELF! When we love someone or something, we are literally bringing the Presence of God into the world. Every time and every person we love supports God's desire to Self-Express! God-as-Love is only interested in giving love to all of its creation.

When you love your work, God goes to work with you. When you love your home, God resides there with you. When you love your partner or spouse, God is present as the love that binds you together. When you love your body, God lives inside of it renewing and regenerating health. Anything and everything you love brings the full Power and Presence of God into being!

Your relationship with Spirit sets the precedence for all other relationships in your life. When you feel in close partnership with God, you are empowered, uplifted and optimistic about life. When you can see the value that God placed in you, and in every person, you become a greater candidate for relationships. Self-value becomes the foundation on which to build healthy, fulfilling relationships. Until you understand the value of your own life, you won't be able to truly value another.

❧ YOU ARE A SPIRITUAL BEING CREATED BY THE ONE SPIRIT

The true essence of your life is the *Spirit* inside your body. Spirit animates and occupies your body—and when it has achieved all that it can or desires in human life, it makes an exit that is as graceful or dramatic as its entrance.

The *Spirit* inside your body is what some people call the "Higher Self" or "Soul." It has no name or particular personality trait, though it is highly individualized. Its agenda is often separate from, and in conflict with your ego. It demands freedom of expression, love and happiness.

Your Spirit is highly creative and insistent upon the fullest expression for your life! It is always looking for windows of opportunity to express itself. It will not be confined in restrictive relationships, careers or bodies. And when it can't find a way out of whatever limitations you may have created in your life, it will begin to create dis-ease or neurosis as an exit strategy.

The way to avoid this destiny is to maintain a life that is joyful, loving and peaceful. Be sure that your relationships are healthy and functional. Create new opportunities for joy to enter your life and compassion to enter your heart. Embrace every opportunity to love. Allow yourself to be moved by your worldly experience. Feel the feelings. Breathe the air. Let your spirit dance if it wants to.

Remember: Your value doesn't come from your body, education, career, money, social status or what kind of neighborhood you live in. It comes from your *Spirit*—and how free it is to love!

GOT LOVE?

Here's a clue for creating healthy relationships: Make love the ONLY purpose for coming together—not guilt, obligation, shared diseases, or biological similarities. Love is a precious gift from our Creator—and it was intended for people who share an honest appreciation for one another.

Don't pretend to have affection for people that you really don't—and for God's sake, don't waste your time with them. Don't go to parties or other social events "just to make an appearance." Don't spend time with relatives out of a sense of guilt or obligation. If you think you're fooling them, you're really not! The heart always knows who favors us and who doesn't.

Love is the ONLY good reason for people to come together—

and the only thing that will truly keep them together. Anything else is pretentious and ungainly. Restore balance to your life and joy to your heart by insisting that love be the only foundation in which to build relationships. Make love the priority in your relationships, not financial, social, or career gains.

After all, you are a perfect expression of God entitled to a life of love and joy! And that's the way God will always see you! You are supposed to be happy and free from suffering. You are not here to pay dues, jump through hoops or prove you are worthy to God. You are here to experience the uniqueness of your own character and express all of the love and joy in your heart. Life is an adventure and you are supposed to be having fun with it!

A Prayer for Love

God is Love and I am love. I was created out of Spirit's desire for Self-expression. I live in this world as a representative of the Divine. Every person I meet holds the same status. We are all equally valuable to God.

Love permeates my awareness, fills my heart—and becomes the magnetic force that draws people into my life. I naturally attract kind and loving people. I draw into my experience people who are generous, affectionate and demonstrative.

My relationships with others are founded in love and respect. I recognize and honor the Divine in them. I see the value they bring to life. Wholeness and balance are at the center of my relationship with others. All of them are functional and joyful.

I love Spirit. I love myself—and I love all of humankind. Together we make up the full pictures of universal love. Thank you God for all of the love that is in my life today— and for the gifts that others bring to my world. Amen.

THE POWER OF THE SERENITY PRAYER

God, grant me the serenity to accept the things I cannot change,
the courage to change the things I can
and the wisdom to know the difference.

This is probably the most effective and necessary prayer when it comes to our relationships with other people. Because, it's easy to forget that we're not here to change them, fix them, or even understand them. We're just here to love them!

Many people misunderstand this. They think that understanding is a prerequisite for loving. They say to the people in their lives: "I just don't understand you!" And they withhold their love until the day they do understand. But that day may never come. People do things that we may never understand—but that's not a valid reason to hold our love hostage. It's easy to love the people we understand. Our challenge is to love the ones we don't!

Acceptance of others always begins first with self-acceptance. Until we accept ourselves in whatever shape or condition we're in, we'll never be able to accept others for what they are. Until we're able to love ourselves in spite of our errors and omissions, we will never completely love another.

Perhaps we should add another sentence to the Serenity Prayer. Maybe it should also read: God, grant me the patience to grow in self-acceptance and the grace to give others the gifts I have withheld from myself.

YOU ARE MORE THAN YOUR HISTORY

Everything that has ever happened to you in this life is recorded in your subconscious mind. Your opinions, feelings, wounds and dreams are all in there—just below the surface of your conscious awareness. And all of it has contributed to who you are today. But, that doesn't mean it has to *limit* you for the rest of your life.

Just because you've survived a rough marriage or an unhappy childhood doesn't make you a survivor. You are a perfect spiritual being created by God. That's who you *really* are. And just because you've been hurt, wounded or betrayed doesn't mean you have to live the rest of your life as a victim. You are a powerful co-creator!

Let the past stay where it belongs—in the past. Don't create tomorrows that look exactly like your yesterdays. Get off the merry-go-round of repetitious living. Your future doesn't have to be a repeat of your past. But in order to change your future, you've got to change your perspective right now.

Look at your life from an entirely different perspective! Just for a minute, forget about your past and think about what you *want* your future to be like. Dream beyond your current limitations. Allow yourself to envision a whole new experience—unlimited by your past experience.

What kind of a person would you be today if nothing bad had ever happened to you? How would you be different if you didn't have to struggle with your current challenge? Take the answers to those questions and start BEING that person now.

You can recreate your future without regard to your past. You can be the person you want to be now. You don't have to move to another town to change your life. You can be the person you want to be, right where you are. Every new day is another opportunity to recreate your life from your best ideas.

✳ DARE TO BE YOURSELF

"The purpose of our lives is to live life. Do not shy away from it, be fearful of it, or deprive yourself of its full enjoyment."
—Dr. Ernest Holmes, *A New Design for Living.*

You are alive at this time in history for a reason. The reason is: The world needs what YOU have to contribute to life. God does not make mistakes. It created you at this time because what you have to give is exactly what the world needs right now.

You were created to be you! Through self-expression, you give the gift of your unique talent to life. You are not here to make a *withdrawal.* You are here to make a *deposit.* You are not here to *get* something good from the world; you're here to *give* something good to the world.

DARE TO BE YOURSELF! Dare to set fear aside and FULLY express who you are. Dare to be different than the crowd. Express the uniqueness of your individuality without fear of non-acceptance. Give the world the *full dose* of your individuality. The world can take it!

Stop trying to "improve" yourself and trust that what Spirit made you to be is good enough! Set yourself free from making comparisons to other people. Know that the path you choose is the *right* one for you. You don't have to dishonor someone else's path in order to validate your own. Enlist in partnership the full creative power of God in creating a life of joyful expression.

❋ Spirit Is Both Creator and Observer

Contrary to the fearful thoughts of many, God did not create life and then abandon it. We have not been left alone to fend for ourselves. We have been set free to discover ourselves. The first rule of spiritual wisdom grants us that God isn't stupid. God is, in fact, a perfect Intelligence that has a huge investment in its creation. And it is intelligent enough to keep a watchful eye on its investments. The universe has not conspired to create consciousness in human beings just as an *experiment.* It has a plan—and an ulterior motive!

The plan is to create *conscious, co-creative partners* who can share the joy of creation: Billions of individual lives all patterned after a perfect Spirit—each one contributing something new to the creation picture. Heaven on earth isn't reserved for a future beyond our time. It is an idea whose time has arrived. We bring Heaven to earth by allowing Spirit full entrance into our lives. And in the process, we become healed. And that healing brings to us a wisdom that our responsibilities lie far beyond our own concerns. In other words, we're not just here to heal ourselves. We're here for God. We're here to bring the full presence of God into the world!

This is not an ego trip. I'm not saying that only *you* can bring God into the world. I'm saying that as each one of us awakens to what we are the presence of God is revealed in the world. When we choose to tap the infinite well of love that we hold inside and give it to those around us, God enters our world. And as billions of people make that choice consciously, Heaven and earth collide.

At times of peak performance, many people experience not only their own presence, but also a sense that *something else* is there with them. It's as though a part of us is "in" the experience—but there's also a part standing aside observing it. That sense is valid.

A part of you is experiencing your life, going through the motions, living as the character "in" the story. But there's also a part of you, your Higher Self or God-AS-you, observing the experience. In other words, Spirit is both Creator and Observer. It creates life so that it can observe it, much the way we do with the things we create. We love to look at our new creations. We look adoringly at them admiring our creative efforts.

Parents are a perfect example of this truth. They love to take pictures of their children. Some of them are obsessive about recording every little achievement. They have volumes of picture albums and videotapes of little Johnny taking his first step and little Suzy riding her first bike. Parents make a huge investment in their children's lives. They give them everything they've got emotionally, spiritually and financially. And they do so without regard to what they'll get in return.

Our relationship with Spirit is similar, except God isn't our parent watching us from a distance. Spirit lives THROUGH us, investing everything it has to offer, observing and *adoring* the life its created AS us.

The key to living a wonderful life is to LET SPIRIT OUT! BE what it wants to be, as you. DO what it wants to do, as you. GO where it wants to go. Follow the lead, listen to the inner urgings, trust the talent and move toward the best idea you've got. You cannot fail!

❈ YOU WERE CREATED FOR SUCCESS

Spirit has given you full authority to decide what you want to do with your life. It designed you with a special talent and gift— and then left you alone to discover who you are. The *talent* is the call. The *gift* is the clue. And it doesn't matter what it is. Colonel Sanders had a talent for making fried chicken. Bob Hope had a gift for making people laugh. And one isn't more valuable than the other.

If by now you still don't know what your talent is, or what gift you've been given—go within and ask. Ask Spirit: *"What do you want to do with my life? What am I supposed to be doing here? What talent have you given me that the world needs right now? Show me the way. Lead me down the right path."*

And keep asking until you receive an answer. The answer *will* come, in time. But how quickly it comes is dependent upon how much "outer noise" you have in your life. Be persistent. There's something valuable you have to give, that the world is in need of. If that weren't true, you wouldn't be alive.

You have everything you need to live a successful life right now! You have a mind that is permanently connected to the only Thinker in the universe—whose intention for your life is success. New ideas rush through your mind daily. The only reason most people's experience of life stays the same from day to day is they keep selecting the same ideas to believe in. The key to creating a brighter future is always in NEW ideas.

Spirit doesn't care whether you're a politician or a plumber. You decide which profession suits your talent. God doesn't have a particular place in mind for you to live. It doesn't care whether you live in L.A. or Omaha. You decide where you want to live. God doesn't know whether you're a Methodist or a Buddhist. You decide which path suits your spiritual needs. God doesn't care whether you're a heterosexual or a homosexual. Your heart will show you who to love.

God's *only* agenda for your life is success! You decide the particulars. Spirit wants the same thing for you that every parent wants for their children: happiness, love, ease, abundance, peace. You have been given the power to co-create whatever you desire. This power was designed to be used only for *constructive* means.

Give your best effort to your best ideas and see what happens. Trust in a power greater than your own. Know that you are not alone in your efforts. You are surrounded by love, empowered by God and guided by wisdom.

After many years of blindly following what society told me I was *supposed* to do to succeed, I stepped out of the mainstream to create my own definition of success. It's a very simple, three-step formula that keeps me on track. Here's my new definition of success:

1. Have fun.
2. Learn something.
3. Help someone along the way.

Have Fun

"Many people feel that God intended them to have a life of suffering and hardship, and is it any wonder that that is what they have?"
—Dr. Ernest Holmes, *A New Design for Living*

God did not create your life as an experience for you to suffer through. Nor was your life designed as an obstacle course that you have to fight your way through. God isn't cruel. It creates out of a desire for Self-expression—just as any great artist does. It creates manifestations of its own perfect ideas. Its only purpose is to express beauty, love and joy.

Your life is supposed to be a joyful experience. You are not here to work hard, climb corporate ladders, or compete for your good. YOUR NUMBER ONE PRIORITY IN LIFE IS TO HAVE FUN!

Surely any Creator that could make a giraffe and an anteater has to have a sense of humor. I have a friend that says, "If just one of the early Renaissance artists had painted a picture with Jesus *smiling*, maybe the Christians wouldn't take everything so seriously."

Statistics show that children laugh dozens of times a day more than adults. I think the reason is as adults, we've lost touch with some of the simple pleasures in life. We've forgotten how to laugh! We've forgotten how to play and have fun. Maybe that's why we're told that in order to enter the kingdom of heaven, we must become as little children. Perhaps, we have to "unlearn" the ways of the world to reenter the center of joy.

Having fun isn't a frivolous activity reserved for goofy people. It is a valid compass that you can use to keep your life on course. If your work is fun, then you're in the right profession. If your relationships are fun, then you're with the right people. If your life is fun, then you're living the right way. Use joy as your compass to keep your life on track. Make "having fun" your number one priority in life.

Learn Something

My number *two* priority in life is to learn something. If I am learning, then I am growing. If I am growing, then I am making progress toward my goals. I never set out to learn. I set out to have fun! Learning is a "by product" of self-expression. As children play, they learn things. But playing is their primary focus. Learning is an *effect* of addressing that concern.

You are not here to learn lessons. Life is not a school and God is not a teacher. You are here to have fun, express joy and unfold the uniqueness of your individual soul. In the process of doing this you will learn new things while achieving your goals.

As you go through life, you may learn many lessons. But remember: All true wisdom comes from within. Experience isn't always the best teacher. A greater wisdom lies waiting on your discovery just underneath the surface of your conscious awareness.

When you need an answer, go *within* and ask Spirit: "Reveal the truth about this person or situation. Tell me what I need to know." And then listen for the answer. It will come.

Help Someone Along the Way

My number *three* priority in life is to help someone along the way. The truth is: Nobody achieves great success on their own. We've all had the help of numerous friends and "unknown angels" to get us where we are today.

We each share the same Spirit. Inside every person is the same Creator. We are ONE life and ONE human family. We have a spiritual obligation to help one another in any way possible. When you help another person achieve their success, both of you are lifted to a higher ground.

The greatest gift you can give to the world is an example of a life well lived. We are all inspired to meet people who know how to forgive quickly and love generously. The world loves a happy person. Seek to BE the person you admire the most and show the world a clear example of success!

Your Appointment with Destiny

Your destiny is strategically linked to every person on the planet. We're all involved in a spiritual evolution of gigantic proportion—that's already started to happen. The change you're going through as you awaken to the discovery that you're more than a physical body reacting to an environment is happening for millions of people around the globe. Spirit-in-us is causing this amazing transformation!

The Infinite Mind that designed the universe created life to evolve. Spirit took form so it could live *consciously* in that form. In other words, the life of God within you is on "automatic pilot" and it is programmed to unfold your Divine potential. It's causing all of the changes that are happening in your experience. And its purpose is to awaken your soul!

Your appointment with destiny has come. The alarm clock is ringing—and it's beckoning you to awaken from your sleep. It's calling you to live differently than you've lived. It's calling your true, authentic self. And once you answer the call, your life will never be the same again.

The Thing You're Looking *For*, Is the Thing You're Looking *With*

Perhaps the transformation that we've waited so long for is already happening *within* us. Maybe what we've spent our whole lives searching for is something each of us already has inside. And the only task we really have is to let it out.

Our lives don't become more loving when we meet the right person. They become more loving when we *let out* the love we have inside—when we find people and things in life we can love, and then *give* our love to them. There's nothing to "acquire" in life that we don't already possess.

Give up trying to change yourself into something you're not. Stop trying to *fix* what's broken or improve what you think is deficient. Spend all of your time revealing your true, authentic self! In doing so, you will be transformed from hateful to loving, from sick to well, from unhealthy to healthy, from poor and weak to rich and strong.

In *The Dance*, author Oriah Mountain Dreamer asks: "What if your contribution to the world and the fulfillment of your own happiness is not dependent upon discovering a better method of prayer or technique of meditation, not dependent upon reading the right book or attending the right seminar, but upon really seeing and deeply appreciating yourself and the world as it is right now?"

Appreciating yourself is not an exercise in ego admiration. It's not a ME, ME, ME agenda. It's a process of uncovering your spiritual nature. It's not about getting what you want from life. It's about creating large spaces in your life for revealing Spirit. If you'll create time in your life for personal reflection, you'll discover new things about yourself. And what you'll discover is that there's a lot of good inside!

True and lasting joy comes from first making that discovery—finding the good inside ourselves, and then learning to appreciate its value. To reveal it on the outside of life, we have to first discover it *within*.

The love you're looking for is the love you already ARE. The joy and happiness you keep trying to get from the world is within you. The wealth you keep trying to find "out there" is the wealth of new ideas that keep vying for your attention.

Stop running around out there desperately looking for the "one thing" that's going to change your life forever. YOU are the "one thing" you've been looking for!

✳ AN IDEA WHOSE TIME HAS COME

"I have a dream that my four children will one day live in a nation where they will not be judged by the color of their skin but by the content of their character.
I have a dream today."

—Martin Luther King, Jr.

Where do our dreams originate? What is the resource for new ideas? From what source did the world's great visionaries gain their insight and vision? Where do advances in technology and science come from? How do we progress as a race?

The answer is: There is only ONE mind in the universe. That mind is the perfect intelligence of Spirit—eternally thinking about what it wants to create. And each individual has access to its ancient wisdom.

All new ideas that advance the human race and move us forward in the world come directly from God. They enter the mind of one woman or man gently urging them to do something about their dreams. Ideas are the currency of the one Thinker in the universe!

In *The Power of Decision* Dr. Raymond Charles Barker wrote: "The Mind of God is a well that never runs dry. All of its ideas are instantly available to you. Ideas seek you out. They need you for their self-expression. Your use of them guarantees your full self-expression. Think of your mind as the birthplace of God's intentions."

We have been designed as co-creative partners in the great drama of life. Spirit dreams great dreams in our hearts. They pass through our minds like trailers of coming attractions at the movies. They rise up from our deep intuitions. They are ideas of what's possible for us and the world we live in. Some of us have the courage to pursue them. Some have the strength to fight for the great vision they've seen in their mind's eye, as did Martin Luther King, Jr. But most people are afraid of the greatness passing through them. They accept the status quo and try to hide from their best ideas, pretending they don't really matter.

You were created by God to dream big dreams! You are *the* way good comes into the world. Your mind was designed as a *receiver;* much like a radio receives the invisible radio waves flowing through the air. Your mind is an outlet for the one Thinker to manifest the good it wants delivered to the world. This is the way God has always entered the world—through the hearts and minds of great men and women.

You are a co-creator, designed to receive great ideas and make them manifest in the world. You are here to bring something good to life. The dreams you call your own, aren't really *yours.* They come from Spirit. They are God's ideas for good in your life. They are coming to you specifically for a reason. That reason is: YOU are the person who is supposed to make something good out of them.

There is nothing more powerful than an idea whose time has come. Take one step toward the best idea you have right now and watch your life be transformed. As you move forward, each new step will be revealed at the right time. All you have to do is take one step at a time—and keep your eye focused on the dream.

BIOGRAPHY

As an ordained minister since 1990, Chris Michaels is the founder and senior minister of the Center for Spiritual Living, a trans-denominational center in Kansas City, Missouri. As an educator, counselor and minister for over thirteen years, he has helped thousands of people understand the basic spiritual principles that govern our lives. His gift of clarity is a rare jewel in a world full of confusion.

As a professional speaker, Chris Michaels is recognized most for his sense of humor and contemporary style. As a counselor, he is best known for his ability to identify the real issue and offer empowering solutions. As a minister, he offers a progressive and authentic format for understanding spiritual principles.

Chris's philosophy is simple and direct, like his speaking style. He believes that each person is on an individual path toward enlightenment—and our soul's greatest assignment is to let out the love we hold inside. Given the proper tools and encouragement, anyone can move beyond the limitations of the past and create the quality of life we are supposed to be living.

ACKNOWLEDGEMENTS

I would like to thank my partner, Aubrey Williams, for putting up with me all of these years and for being a constant inspiration for love and the "trinity alliance" for all of the prayer support. Without a "chance" meeting with Lisa Hepner, this book would have never been possible. Thank you, Lisa, for your patience and gentle guidance through the creative process. My friend Victoria Moran's contribution was priceless. Thank you, Victoria, for always seeing my value. And of course, I want to thank Dr. Richard Carlson for his glowing review of the book and Bense Garza for the cover design. I am truly blessed to have collaborated with such high quality individuals. God bless you all.

ORDER INFORMATION

For more copies of *Your Soul's Assignment* please call or send a check or money order to the address below.

Awakening World Enterprises (A.W.E)
1621 West 50th Street
Kansas City, MO 64112
(816) 931-9277

Feel free to check out the website below:

www.yoursoulsassignment.com